LOST IN AUSTIN

LOST IN AUSTIN

A NEVADA MEMOIR

Jim Andersen

UNIVERSITY OF NEVADA PRESS RENO & LAS VEGAS

University of Nevada Press, Reno, Nevada 89557 USA
Copyright © 2009 by James William Andersen
All rights reserved
Manufactured in the United States of America
Design by Kathleen Szawiola

Library of Congress Cataloging-in-Publication Data
Andersen, Jim (James William), 1944–
Lost in Austin : a Nevada memoir / Jim Andersen.
p. cm.
ISBN 978-0-87417-787-9 (pbk. : alk. paper)
1. Andersen, Jim (James William), 1944–
2. Austin (Nev.)—Biography.
3. Austin (Nev.)—Social life and customs.
4. Austin (Nev.)—History.   I. Title.
F849.A9A535   2009   979.3'33—dc22
[B]   2009015666

The paper used in this book is a recycled stock made from
30 percent post-consumer waste materials, certified by FSC,
and meets the requirements of American National Standard
for Information Sciences—Permanence of Paper
for Printed Library Materials, ANSI/NISO Z39.48-1992 (R2002).
Binding materials were selected for strength and durability.

FIRST PRINTING
18   17   16   15   14   13   12   11   10   09
5   4   3   2   1

To God for dragging me,
kicking and screaming,
away from my deserved fate,
and bringing me
Val and Withanee

Contents

LOST IN AUSTIN

LIKE IT IS

Austin Township Courtroom

"All rise."

The court clerk steps out of the doorway and to the side so the judge can walk past to his elevated desk.

"Austin Justice Court is now in session."

I chuckle inwardly, as I always do. Not at the clerk, or the court, or the ritual, but at me. How on earth did I end up here?

I sit down in the high-backed judge's chair, being careful not to get tangled up in my robe, and say, "Thank you. Be seated."

They obediently sit down, "they" being the district attorney, the defendant and his attorney, and—behind the ornate wooden railing that is known as the bar—the witnesses who have been subpoenaed, along with a few spectators.

There is no uncertainty about who wears the Big Kahuna hat around here; it is I, and the silence is complete, waiting for myself to speak.

Could this have happened anywhere but Austin? Maybe.

But I doubt it.

Austin Township

Like people, towns are unique. You usually have to live in one for a while to discover what it is that sets it apart from any other place in the world, but it'll eventually surface. Some towns only give up their particular flavor grudgingly, but a few, like Austin, are immediately recognized as unique, which is the exact word that comes to mind the moment you see it.

I'm not the only one who thinks so. The author Oscar Lewis published a book in 1953 titled *The Town That Died Laughing*, which is about Austin, Nevada. He noticed that while a lot of Austin had indeed died laughing, some of it was still breathing—mainly, he believed, because Austin was the governmental seat of the County of Lander, State of Nevada, and was therefore immortal in the sense that somebody has to keep the paperwork flowing. It follows, then, that when that prop was pulled out, when the county seat was actually moved ninety-two miles north to Battle Mountain in 1978, Austin would have the permanence of a canvas chair in a high wind.

However, as they say in middle school, that was, like, decades ago, and Austin is still here, alive and well. And laughing.

Me too.

Today, Austin itself is home to about 250 people, give or take. There are another 800 or so in the township, which includes the southern 2,500 square miles of Lander County. The official 2000 census lists fewer people, but it is wrong. I can attest to that because I wasn't counted, nor was my family, and there's no telling how many others. My wife and I didn't even notice, until we compared notes one day about what kind of questions the census takers asked on their survey and found out neither of us had been approached. Since we're not exactly low profile—I'm the judge, my wife's a schoolteacher, and my daughter's a student—and we live right smack in the middle of town, perhaps they were in a hurry to get back to civilization and skipped a few houses on their way out. Or, more probably, they momentarily became as laid back as the rest of us and just missed a few.

What can I say? It happens.

Most of the people who live in town own businesses on Main Street, which doubles as Highway 50, or work in public-sector jobs. Others have as many as three or four part-time jobs that they string together to make ends meet, and some do seasonal work, such as construction, and live in Austin between jobs.

A recent spate of semiretired folks, sick to weary death of city life, have adopted Austin as their home, as I once did, and just enjoy being out here in the exact center of nowhere.

It's a good center too, and a great nowhere—none better, if you ask me—

and it takes people who weren't born here a long time to find it. You have to take Highway 50 right into the heart of Nevada. Not many people are inclined to do that, once they look at a road map and see how far it is between gas stations. *Sunset* magazine even dubbed this stretch of highway "the loneliest road in America," and urged drivers to be current on their survival skills before taking it. I find that kind of flattering, thank you, but then, what Los Angeles native wouldn't?

Austin lies 70 miles west of Eureka—a boom-or-bust mining town that is currently booming to the tune of perhaps eight hundred souls—and 112 miles east of Fallon.

Fallon is where we do most of our shopping, as they have a Wal-Mart and a Pizza Hut, not to mention things like banks and dentists. Close to ten thousand people live in Fallon in a comparatively mild climate, which, when you factor in all the services available, is why a lot of us tend to gravitate there when we get too old, or too tired, to fight Austin's winters.

Two other state routes intersect Highway 50 near Austin; State Route 305 goes north 92 miles to Battle Mountain and State Route 376 connects with Tonopah, 115 miles south. Older maps will show these highways as 8A North and 8A South, using Highway 50 as a sort of Mason-Dixon Line separating the two. Therefore, for all practical purposes, there are four highways that can take you to Austin. Or away from it, depending on your particular frame of mind. An occasional bout of winter cabin fever can influence that, by the way, and 8A South starts looking pretty good around February.

Unlike most Nevada towns, which are built in flat desert country, Austin is in the mountains. At an elevation of 6,600 feet it is higher than Lake Tahoe, and the air is noticeably thin if you're visiting from sea level.

Traveling eastbound, Highway 50 climbs into town from Reese River Valley through Pony Canyon. The highway stays in the bottom of the canyon all the way through town and then hairpins left as it leaves. From there it snakes up the side of the Toiyabe Mountains to Austin Summit at an elevation of 7,500 feet.

Most of the houses in Austin are terraced up the hillsides to the north, and the farther up you go, the better view you have. It's kind of like stadium seating; everybody can see out above the home in front, the only difference being one of perspective, though when you get off the canyon floor the view opens up and takes in Reese River Valley several hundred feet below.

There are relatively few level roads and some that are awful steep, which makes for good sledding on snowy days, whether you're on a sled or not.

Austin is a little sparse on services these days, having lost its grocery store several years ago. Of all the losses, including the county seat, the grocery store was probably the most mourned. True, in its latter days week-old stuff was the best you could hope for, but at least canned goods and magazines were within arm's reach, so to speak. Thank goodness our gas stations put in minimarts, so we can get by between trips to Fallon, but it gets rough sometimes.

We do have a hardware store that is surprisingly well stocked, and there are several new shops on Main Street that were vacant buildings not too long ago, so we're doing all right.

In exchange for what we get in return, which are admittedly intangibles in the way of peace and quiet and quality of life, we're getting the best of the deal, no doubt about it.

And besides that, the judge here is about the nicest guy you'd ever want to meet. Unless, of course, I've retired by the time this book comes out.

LIKE IT WAS

Jedediah Smith, an early mountain man, was best known for having killed a grizzly bear with a knife in the Rockies after the clearly unsociable creature tore his scalp off. Following that, the Great Basin of Nevada certainly wouldn't hold any terrors for him.

Smith was the first white man of record to explore the area, passing through about a hundred miles south of present-day Austin in 1827. He left scant mention of that leg of his journey but did note that "Some isolated mountains rise from this plain of sand, to the regions of perpetual snow."

That's not too bad a description even today, except for the parts about the mountains being isolated and the snow being perpetual. The Great Basin Desert, which includes all of central Nevada, is characterized by north-south mountain ranges separated by wide, desolate valleys. It really is a basin in that water that comes in, stays in. There is no outlet, and waterways eventually either drain into lakes, as does the Walker River, or just call it quits and sink into the desert, like the Humboldt River.

Eighteen years after Smith's trip, in 1845, John C. Frémont came through and described the general area as a "massive land of internal drainage . . . that cannot be less than four or five hundred miles each way." He didn't seem overly impressed either, adding: "It is called a desert and, from what I saw of it, sterility may be its prominent characteristic."

For some reason, these reports didn't stir much interest in the area.

It took another fourteen years, until 1859, for yet another explorer to come through. Captain James Hervey Simpson was commissioned by the U.S. Army to find a route between settlements in Utah and the Carson Valley, and he pioneered the Central Overland Trail, which became the Overland Stage route across Nevada. The short-lived Pony Express used the same general route but took several shortcuts that weren't suitable for wagons. Both crossed the Toiyabe Mountains near Emigrant Pass, three miles north of present-day Austin, and both maintained stations along the route.

One of the stage stops, located at Jacobs Springs near the Reese River, gave rise to the town of Jacobsville. Jacobsville was designated the first seat of Lander County, which accounted for a third of Nevada Territory at the time. Today the site is marked only by a historical sign on the north side of Highway 50 five miles west of Austin.

Among the employees of the stage line at Jacobs Springs in 1862 was an agent by the name of William Talcott. By his account, some horses got away from the station and ran off into the mountains. He followed them into what would become known as Pony Canyon in the Toiyabe Mountains, where he "accidentally" found a ledge of silver ore. Although that tale has always sounded a little artificial to me, the rest, as they say, is history.

The fledgling county seat of Jacobsville was too far away from the mines that soon developed in Pony Canyon, so the settlement of Clifton sprang up right at the mouth of the canyon. The steep-walled canyon itself was deemed unsuitable for a town site, at least at that particular moment. A couple of months of climbing up to the mines from the valley floor, however, changed a few minds, and before long a road was built and the whole shebang was carried up into the canyon, where Austin was founded. Both Clifton and Jacobsville quickly went into decline.

In the manner of all mining boomtowns, Austin grew by leaps and bounds almost overnight, topping out in 1864 at well over six thousand souls, making it the second-largest city in Nevada, behind only Virginia City. If you stand on a hillside today and try to imagine six thousand people living and working and playing in this canyon, I guarantee you won't be able to do it. The nineteenth-century equivalent of the Las Vegas Strip, right here in Pony Canyon? Nah.

Still, there it was. A lot of the buildings on Main Street today were built during those heyday years, and from their design and construction you certainly get a sense of the up-and-coming-city attitude that gripped the planners. Austin was no flash in the pan, nosiree bob. And you know, if they hadn't built it to last, it probably wouldn't have. There is a line from a movie that says, "If you build it they will come," to which Austin's founders might have added, "If you build it well, they will stay."

Nothing remains of Clifton, but the site is just below Austin on the level expanse of ground that today holds the rodeo grounds and petroleum bulk plant.

Several years ago, while I was working at the bulk plant—well, actually I was taking a break from working at the bulk plant, kind of like William Talcott when he found the silver, I think—I noticed a blackened object sticking out of the ground. It turned out to be the end of a disintegrating old leather belt, and when I unearthed the whole thing it was, in fact, a gun belt complete with bullet loops and a holster. It was held together by, and decorated heavily with, copper rivets, not entirely unlike the toy six-gun sets I played with as a kid. Unfortunately there weren't enough rivets to hold all the atoms together, and the ravages of time and weather resulted in the belt falling apart even as I lifted it. It was enough, and you can take this to the bank, to make a grown man cry.

To the east of the bulk plant, right at the mouth of the canyon, is a shooting range, the home of the Pony Canyon Gun Club. In the 1880s the site was the southern terminus of the Nevada Central Railroad, and the town depot was located there. The Nevada Central was a narrow-gauge railway built to haul silver ore, freight, and passengers between Austin and the Central Pacific rail terminal at Battle Mountain, ninety-two miles north. During the final phase of construction, with the builders under a strict deadline to finish the tracks to Austin by midnight of February 9, 1880, it became obvious they weren't going to make it in time, which would result in a catastrophic loss of funding. To resolve the problem, the city fathers met in emergency session and simply extended the city limits out to meet the tracks.

That's the sort of thing that makes me proud to be an American.

You can almost hear the next thought from way back then: While it was nice to have rail service to old Clifton, wouldn't it be swell to bring it on up into town?

So tracks were laid up to Austin and right down the center of Main

Street all the way through town. The initial climb up from the valley floor included grades of over 7 percent, however, and was thought to be too steep for steam engines, so mule teams were used to pull the cars up at first. But when someone finally tried a locomotive it came up right up the slope like the little engine that could, and the mules were released from duty. The locomotive pulling the Austin City Railway into town from Clifton was thereafter known as the Mules Relief.

William Talcott's silver discovery, of course, was what brought all this into being. His initial assay showed the ore to be worth $7,000 per ton, over twice what the best Comstock ore had assayed. That's all it took to set off one of the biggest silver rushes in the West, with thousands of would-be millionaires flocking to the newly formed Reese River Mining District. As often happened, most of the prospectors who made money from Austin's silver rush did so by staking claims in the early stages and then selling them to conglomerates that eventually did the mining. The nearly insurmountable advantage of thus being among the first to reach a silver strike was what caused the all-out, no-holds-barred race to every new discovery. Because it was difficult, if not impossible, for a lone prospector to extract silver from the ore, most of the late arrivals left for greener pastures, and Austin quickly lost a good portion of the initial population surge. In truth, the silver boom never did live up to its billing.

Some of the scams sure did, though. One of the finest to hit the stock market was the impressive-sounding Reese River Navigation Company, formed to ship the mountains of silver out by barge, down the Reese River. Obviously unbeknownst to the investors, that particular waterway had only been promoted to a river upon the arrival of Captain Simpson in 1859, who named it after his guide, John Reese. The Shoshone Indians who lived there just called it "Fish Creek," which was still an exaggeration. It's seldom more than three or four feet wide, and maybe a foot deep. There may not have been any suckers associated with the Reese River until the stock was put on the market, but afterward there were several schools of 'em.

Even though these schemes were routinely unmasked, there seemed to be no shortage of investors willing to gamble on the highly publicized strike, and the money kept rolling in. This did in fact enable several mines to improve their milling procedures, and they eventually worked out more effective ways of separating the silver from the sulfides, a problem that had always been something of a nightmare. Although refining it was expensive, the ore was so rich the mines could still turn a profit, and mining fueled Austin's economy for the rest of the century.

Meanwhile, back on Main Street . . .

Because Austin's Main Street ran along the very bottom of Pony Canyon, runoff from rainstorms was a problem. Water from the upper reaches of the canyon, with no place else to drain, accumulated on the way down and resulted in flash floods running through the middle of town. Early photographs show the aftermath of these surges, which often left several inches of mud covering the street, along with the debris associated with high, fast-moving water, including boulders bigger than kitchen chairs. It was such a common occurrence that two-story buildings hinged their outdoor staircases at the top, so that the end resting on the ground could be pulled up out of the way of floods by means of a rope. They were known as "swinging staircases," and many survived well into the twentieth century. The last one was finally replaced by a regular structure in the 1990s.

Another innovation involved draining the water quickly from the flat-roofed businesses lining the street. Rectangular drain holes were left in the false fronts, with wooden flumes carrying water away from the roofs before it could accumulate. The flumes angled downward onto Main Street and discharged even more water into the floods. In the winter months ice often built up in the flumes, causing a hazard to anyone who happened beneath them when the ice broke loose.

The topography of Pony Canyon hasn't changed since William Talcott found silver, but Austin today has an adequate drainage system from one end of town to the other. In spite of that, water from heavy rainstorms still gathers enough momentum coming down the hillsides to scatter debris across even the best-drained roadways.

Personally speaking, every year a good portion of our property washes down into Overland Street, and every year a good portion of the hillside above washes down onto our lots, so by spreading it around we break even. I don't imagine it was any different 150 years ago, and it would appear that, given enough time, Austin will eventually end up out in the valley.

Austin became the seat of Lander County almost by default, as much of the populations of both Jacobsville and Clifton migrated to the booming canyon. An election in 1863, which made it official, was more or less a technicality. And when Nevada went from a territory to full statehood in October of the following year, that only increased the importance of county government in the general scheme of things.

As soon as the election was in the books, work began on Austin's two-story county courthouse. It was constructed of brick, with large slabs of hand-hewn granite hoisted into place for windowsills. When it was finished the upstairs contained two county offices, the judge's chambers, and a large courtroom complete with twelve-man jury seating. The ground floor housed the rest of the county offices, the sheriff, and the jail.

Of note is the small second-story courthouse balcony. In 1881 one Richard Jennings was taken forcibly from the jail in the wee hours of the morning and lynched from the balcony's convenient metal railing. An article in the next day's newspaper suggested that bad men might want to give Austin a wide berth, lest they fall to "Jennings' rawhide lariat."

In an earlier, more traditional, hanging, Rufus Anderson was tried and sentenced to death in 1868. A scaffold was erected in front of the courthouse, the noose tied around the prisoner's neck, the trapdoor opened, and the knot came loose, dropping Rufus—who was obviously having a bad day anyway—to the ground below. It was tried a second time, and again the knot came loose, and again Rufus plummeted to the ground. Undeterred, the sheriff hauled him up once again and this time tied him to a chair, possibly because Rufus was unable to stand upright at that point. The third time's the charm, as they say, and the hapless Rufus finally met his end.

Richard Jennings must have known the story of the triple-hanging of Rufus a few years before, and you have to wonder if he wasn't a little relieved that a mob came for him instead.

On the other side of the coin, Austin also produced three of the finest churches in the state. The first Catholic church built in Nevada, St. Augustine's, still sits on the corner of Court and Virginia streets in Austin. It's now in private hands and is being restored, but until the mid-1980s it was still used for services. The Methodist church has also been restored and is currently the Austin Town Hall. It sits above Main on Court Street about two blocks east of the Catholic church, and these are the two churches you see up on the hills when you first enter town from the west. The Episcopal church is on Main Street next to the Toiyabe Cafe and is the only one of the three that is still active. A built-in pipe organ provides music for Sunday services, as it has since the Civil War. All three have steeples and bell towers, and all three reflect the grandest architecture of the period.

Austin's early years were peppered with individuals whose exploits could, and sometimes did, garner the attention of the entire nation. Reuel Colt Gridley was among the first. Reuel was a grocer in upper Austin who backed the Democratic ticket in the town's first mayoral election in 1864. He made a wager with a Republican friend that whichever of them turned out to be on the losing side would have to carry a fifty-pound sack of flour from one end of town to the other. When the votes were counted Reuel had lost, so he made good on the bet and, to the accompaniment of the town band playing "John Brown's Body," carried the bag on his shoulder the length of Main Street. When he finished, someone suggested he auction off the sack of flour and donate the proceeds to the Sanitary Fund, a fledgling organization dedicated to providing aid to wounded civil war veterans. Mr. Gridley did so, and the spirited bidding finally ended at $250. But the Gridley sack of flour wasn't destined to become pancakes yet, not by a long shot. The winning bidder returned the flour to be reauctioned, which it was, again and again throughout the day, until some three hundred people had briefly owned the sack, paying out a total of $8,000. And in the end, Gridley still had the flour.

A decade earlier that surely would have been the end of it, but with the telegraph now in place, word spread at the speed of light, and Virginia City—Austin's archrival in those days—sent back this message, as reported by Mark Twain in his book *Roughing It:* "Fetch along your flour sack!"

Gridley immediately did, and from there the unanticipated consequence of a *losing* bet snowballed into a nationwide tour for the Sanitary Fund, which eventually turned into the American Red Cross. By the time the dust settled, Gridley and his famous sack of flour had raised nearly a quarter of a million dollars.

Unfortunately, this whirlwind tour cost Reuel Gridley his health, and his absence from his store in Austin cost him his business. He moved to California, and although there are conflicting accounts of his life following relocation, a monument to Reuel Colt Gridley now stands in a Stockton, California, cemetery.

Another Austin transplant, Emma Nevada, was a world-famous opera singer in the late 1800s, routinely touring Europe and performing before royalty. She never forgot the childhood home in Austin where she grew up as Emma Wixom and sang in the church, though, and she returned to Austin in 1885 for a brief performance to show her gratitude.

The house where Emma grew up was on the northeast corner of Water and 7th streets and was listed as the Emma Nevada House on walking-tour brochures. It was lived in until a couple of years ago but was then torn down to make way for the modern house that sits there now.

An eastern financier named Anson Phelps Stokes passed through Austin in the 1860s and took an immediate liking to the area, much as I would more than a hundred years later. He invested heavily in Austin's Manhattan Company, which did well for him, and he went on to play a major role in building the Nevada Central Railroad. Although silver was starting its decline, in 1891 Stokes formed the Austin Mines Company and began work on the Clifton Tunnel project, which burrowed beneath Lander Hill for a distance of a mile. It was intended to drain the shafts of water, in the manner of the more famous Sutro Tunnel in Virginia City, and thereby lower the costs of getting the ore out. It worked, too, when it was completed in 1896, and a new mill at Clifton went into operation in 1898 to take advantage of the reduced costs, but silver prices never bounced back and it turned out to be the last gasp for silver mining in Austin.

In the meantime, a mile south of Austin, overlooking the valley, Stokes built a castle. Completed in 1897, it was constructed of hand-hewn granite and modeled after a castle Phelps had seen in Italy. However, if your vision of a castle is a turreted, walled fortress with drawbridge and moat, you're probably not going to recognize this one right away. I've described it before as a stone shoebox stood on end, and I believe I'll stick with that, although I've since heard the structure referred to as a "medieval tower," which is probably closer to the mark. However you choose to label it, there is no argument that its construction took some doing. It is three stories tall and was fairly intact even into the 1950s, when, in the interests of safety for curiosity seekers, the inside was stripped and the staircases removed.

The one constant in Austin throughout its heyday and right on up into the late twentieth century was a newspaper, the *Reese River Reveille*. It made its debut in May of 1863 and survived for more than 120 years, at one point attaining the distinction of being the oldest continuously published newspaper in Nevada. The *Reveille* has, like the town itself, made a comeback recently and is now published quarterly by Main Street Shops of Austin, with Linda Seymour as its editor.

The old *Reese River Reveille*, which is archived in a vault in the assessor's office at the courthouse, is so filled with the essence of yesteryear that it's almost impossible to get any research done. I get so caught up in the new mercantile opening, or the deluge of the latest storm, or the shooting of a citizen Monday last, that I forget what I came in for. The printed word from back then seems stilted and deliberately formal, as I imagine ours will appear a century from now, but once you get into the rhythm of it your mind sort of slips away. It's like stepping into a low-end time machine.

Speaking of which, let's all step together now across the decades into Austin as it was when I arrived in 1974, which was a lot different than it was before or is now:

All of the county offices—that is, the assessor, the clerk, the treasurer, the auditor, the recorder, and the sheriff—were housed in the courthouse, along with their associated records since the town was founded. A new sheriff's building was under construction on the lots just east of the courthouse, so that department was packing up and getting ready to move, but the rest of the courthouse business was being carried on just as it had been for a hundred years. The courtroom itself was on the second floor, along with the judge's chambers, and was the domain of District Court rather than the justice of the peace because Austin was the county seat. Although I wasn't personally involved in any court proceedings until after District Court, along with the rest of the county offices, was moved to Battle Mountain, it's my understanding that Justice Court was allowed to use the courtroom when the higher court wasn't in session. The Austin justice of the peace inherited the courtroom and the judge's chambers after the move, which I would later come to regard as a fine reason to get rid of the county seat. The other elected county officials, who up until then had lived in Austin, never did come to appreciate that logic.

Across Main Street from the courthouse stood the Nevada National Bank, housed in a single-wide mobile home modified to hold a large vault secured by a massive iron door equipped with wheeled locking bolts—a safe that would make Scrooge McDuck envious. An alarm system was wired into the budding sheriff's office across the way, just in case. A would-be burglar later broke *into* the sheriff's office to disarm the bank system in the wee hours of the morning, which he did with a burglar's efficiency. He was, however, unable to actually get into the bank, so he stole a Forest Service pickup that he promptly wrecked in the curves below town. Undeterred, he came back and stole another car, which he also wrecked in the curves below town. Finding himself without the necessary skills to make good an escape, he was discovered late that afternoon hiding in the bell tower of St. Augustine's Catholic Church, apparently hoping for one of those miracles you sometimes hear about. If anybody ever needed one, he certainly did.

The bank changed hands a couple of times, eventually closing down in the late 1980s for lack of business. It is typical in Austin that when a job evaporates, the displaced worker finds something else to do, usually within a couple of days. Shortly after the closure, the unemployed longtime banker found herself working as a waitress at the Toiyabe Cafe, wherein one of the local patrons was heard to remark to his fellow diners, "Count your change; old habits die hard."

The Austin Clinic occupies the bank building now, using the vault as what is probably the most secure drug cabinet in the United States.

The first building down from the clinic was the Austin Garage, headquarters for the Austin Light and Power Company. Until Sierra Pacific took over, the Austin Power Company supplied the town with electricity. Two gigantic diesel engines were housed in the garage, one of which was always powering the generators. I owned the Stagecoach Inn, two buildings down from the garage, and you could feel the diesel engines throbbing through the sidewalk like sailors can feel a ship's engine through the deck. The actual sound seemed muted and hardly noticeable, but the day they turned those diesels off was startling in its quietness.

Between the Stagecoach Inn and the Austin Garage sits the two-story

Masonic Hall. It's been in use since just short of forever and is still in use today.

Downhill of the Stagecoach was Carol's Country Store, later Carol's Country Kitchen, now Main Street Shops. Beyond was, and still is, Lander Lumber. Today it's a hardware store that no longer sells lumber, but the name Lander Lumber was too darn catchy to get rid of.

On the corner next to the lumberyard was an old brick building that carried the faint lettering "Silver Dollar Bar." It is now a vacant lot.

Across Virginia Street from that vacant lot is another one. Until 1978 it held the old Austin Hotel. The second floor of the venerable brick building housed the hotel rooms and a hardwood dance floor that was said to be anchored on large springs. A saloon and connecting restaurant occupied the ground floor, which is where the fire broke out that destroyed all but the bar. On my first visit to Austin—a baking July afternoon—I stopped in at the saloon for a cold brew, one with icy frost sliding down off the mug. Entering the dimly lit bar was like walking into a paneled cave, but once my eyes adjusted I was impressed with how polished the place looked. The bartender was an older gentleman wearing slacks, a pressed white shirt, and black bow tie, which even then was rare to see anymore. His name was Jess Smith, "Smitty" for short, and although I only met him that one time, I've never forgotten him. You could see he'd been around the block a few times, but it hadn't dimmed his outlook at all. Smitty was Austin personified and, like the town, he made you feel at home.

Clara's Golden Club was just down the street from the Austin Hotel. Clara herself, a white-haired grandmother, ran the place most nights and doubled as the dealer at her blackjack table. Many's the time I'd ask for a card and she'd peek at her cards, look dubious, and say, "Are you sure you want to do that?" Curiously, I never did lose big at Clara's table.

The building on the end of the block, the one with the bell tower, was originally the fire station. It was vacant when I arrived and has since been converted to Austin's youth center, which probably isn't the best place to have a bell tower with an operable loud bell. The new fire station is up the street next to the courthouse.

Across Cedar Street from the youth center is the International Hotel.

The whole building, along with the furnishings, was disassembled from its original site in Virginia City and carried to Austin board by board, where it was reassembled. Hotel rooms were on the second floor, while the ground floor housed a bar and, in 1974, a Chinese restaurant. Art and Faye Yan ran the place, and the cook was a Chinaman known as "Flash." I never learned if that was his real name, though I doubt it. Flash played keno whenever he went to the big city, and every now and then he came back with a brand-new, big, expensive car. It was rumored he had a keno system that, in fact, worked. I never saw anything that would cause me to think otherwise.

The next block down, on the corner of Main and Pine streets, was the site of Kittie Bonner's house. It's been gone for many years, but I remember it as a red, sprawling, ranch-type house encompassed by a covered porch. She had a barber's chair in the front room and gave haircuts, while at the same time weaving some pretty good tales.

Beyond Kittie's house was a vacant motel, and at the very end of town was a Texaco gas station, owned at the time by Jim and Maggie Helming. It burned to the ground in 1985 and was never rebuilt.

If you turn around there and start back up the street, everything was the same as it is now until you get past the motels. Then there was a clothing and sundry shop named merely "The Shoppe," next to the large brick IML building.

IML was a freight line, and their trucks used to deliver and pick up freight in Austin on a regular schedule. Lawrence Saralegui was the local agent, and if you had something come in he'd either find you and let you know or deliver it himself. IML usually hauled heavy stuff, like grader blades or drill steel for mining companies. If your order would fit on a mail truck, they probably wouldn't bother with it.

Next to the IML building stood Vigus's Market. Ed and Louise Vigus sold everything from groceries to fishing tackle, but the part I liked best was the meat counter. You could order as much lunch meat or cheese as you liked, and Ed would slice it up for you and wrap it in thick white butcher's paper. The market changed hands a couple of times after Ed and Louise passed away, eventually closing down in the 1990s.

Next to the old market is the Owl Club, a bar that in 1974 was Betty's Bar. If you look at the front of it, though, you'll see a resemblance, perhaps, to the movie theater it once was, where they sold tickets from a window set in an angled wall, across from a similar wall that held movie posters. To get into the bar today you walk up the same ramp as moviegoers once did.

On the east corner of the block is another bar, Dessie and Mary's Saloon, which was, sequentially, the Black Cat, succeeded by Vance and Arlene's Saloon.

The Trading Post, across Virginia Street, used to be Casady's Chevron Station. Whit Skinner was running it when I arrived, and they had a newspaper article hanging on the wall reporting the station's absolutely unheard-of employment of a *female service station attendant,* right here in the little town of Austin, Nevada! Holy moly!

A block up from Casady's sits the Toiyabe Cafe, which grew out from the Toiyabe Drive-In. The inside dining room was added in the late 1970s and later expanded again, but the existing counter is where the outside order window used to be. Not surprisingly, the drive-in always closed for the snowy months, which had to have taken a healthy cut out of the outfit.

Across Main Street you'll now find the Senior Citizens Center. When it opened, around 1975, I was involved in starting up the Stagecoach Inn Restaurant and wasn't especially happy to see the government getting into the restaurant business. Because traffic on Highway 50 drops off so sharply in the late autumn, we barely survived our first winters as it was.

The new post office up the street was completed in 1968, long before I arrived, replacing the original that was located next to the Austin Hotel.

Across the street from the post office was the county road department, whose employees plowed the roads in the winter and repaired potholes in the summer. Not that there were all that many potholes to fix, since the only paved road in 1974 was Main Street, also known as Highway 50. The Austin Volunteer Ambulance Service occupies the property now, having moved there from their niche at the fire station after the county road department took over the grounds of the state highway department, a block farther east, when the state moved to their newly built station a quarter mile north of town in the 1980s. It was like musical chairs without the chairs. Or the music.

Bert Gandolfo Park, completed in 1978, sits a block east of the county road department and consists of a playground and picnic area, a swimming pool, horseshoe pits, and a baseball field. Bert was a county commissioner from Austin who was largely responsible for getting the park built, which was about the last county project funded outside of the soon-to-be county seat of Battle Mountain. Before the park was put in, the eastern terminus of the Mules Relief railway, consisting of a lone wooden building, sat where center field of the ballpark is today.

Across from the park is the Baptist church with its accompanying RV Park, a curious combination to be sure, but one Joseph and Mary would have appreciated the night the inn was full.

The one-story stone building east of the church is the Gridley Store, now a museum but just a vacant building in 1974. It dates to 1863, when it housed the business of the same Reuel Gridley who carried his flour sack to fame.

Finally, at the end of town sits the T-Rix Mountain Bike Shop. The buildings used to house Lombardo Milling and Mining, which operated the Little Bluebird Turquoise Mine in the Shoshone Mountains twenty-five miles west. Across Highway 50 is a wrecking yard and mechanic shop belonging to Ray and Irene Salisbury.

It is possible to get a peek of Austin as it was in 1970 via the silver screen. In *Vanishing Point*, Barry Newman, playing a strung-out driver chased by inept cops, speeds westbound over Austin Summit and down into town, where he angles from the highway onto Overland Street in front of Gridley's Store. The chase continues down Overland to Water Street, then past the pristine St. Augustine's Church, where Barry skids around the corner onto Virginia Street, and back down to Highway 50. He, and the police, barely make the corner in front of the old Austin Hotel, speed through the rest of town—maybe two second's worth—and turn right on State Route 305. At the junction there the pursuit vehicle rolls, and the now-dehorsed deputy radios that the fugitive is headed south to Tonopah.

Tonopah? I hate to tell them, but the fugitive turned north to Battle Mountain.

No wonder they couldn't catch him.

How to Get Here

Ｉf you live in a city, it's not easy to move to the country. Even if you hate your job, and hate the traffic, and hate waiting in line, and hate the noise and the rush and the smog, it's not easy. I know people who hated it even more than I did, yet they elected to stay where they were because leaving is just so darn hard.

I'd been married for four years in 1974 and had lived in Antioch, a medium-sized northern California city not far east of San Francisco Bay, since 1966. The last of Marlys's kids graduated from high school in 1974, so there was no reason to stay. Well, except for our jobs, of course. Marlys was a secretary in the front offices at Crown Zellerbach's big paper mill in Antioch. I was a journeyman welder in the maintenance shop at the same mill. She'd been there nine years, I'd been there eight. Since you needed ten years to be vested in Crown's retirement program, the smart move was to tough it out a couple more years. But the gas crunch of '73 had been the final straw. We could buy gas for our cars only on even-numbered days of the month because our license plates both ended in an even numbers, and the lines at the station were excruciatingly long. While waiting in line, my mind would invariably drift away to Austin, Nevada.

We'd stumbled onto Austin by accident. Because of California's horrible tax structure, along with its myriad laws and regulations and codes that kept your imagination bolted firmly in place, we looked at Nevada. No personal income tax and low property taxes got high marks from us. Very high marks. We didn't want to move out of the city into another city, though, no matter what, so out came the maps.

The first 1973 trip was focused on towns along Interstate 80 in northern Nevada. Those towns didn't work for us at all, so out came the maps again. For the second trip, well, Caliente looked promising and off the beaten path. The name means "hot" in Spanish, and it was small. I stopped in Carson City to get gas—in Nevada it didn't matter what my license plate number read—and when I told the attendant I was headed to Caliente he offhandedly remarked, "Got someone in the prison there, do you?"

Prison? Turns out it was a really a juvenile detention facility, but still, no thanks.

So we took Highway 50 east instead, through Fallon, which was nice but too big, and thence to points east. A couple of miles beyond the small cafe/bar/gas station of Middlegate, we turned off onto a looping detour—State Route 722—that used to be the original Highway 50, hoping we might see some coyotes or wild horses or cowboys or flying saucers. The high desert country was so appealing, so lonely, so vast, so . . . *outside,* that you knew something remarkable had to be lurking just around the corner.

When we got to Smith Creek Dry Lake, the map showed a dirt road turning off to the right that crossed the Shoshone Mountains and inter- sected a road that was shown to run alongside a river: the Reese River, signified by a blue line on my official Rand McNally road atlas. Naturally, with visions of rope swings dangling from tree limbs above Old Man River, we turned right.

Our road dead-ended at the county road, just like the map said, and we sat there, confused, as the cloud of alkali dust we'd churned up drifted slowly past the car. There was the valley, yes, apparently the Reese River Valley, but there was no river. No river, and no trees or willows to indicate a river. Nothing but sagebrush and greasewood as far as the eye could see, all the way to the Toiyabe Mountain Range rising against the sky several miles distant.

What a fine nonkettle of fish this was.

But as often happens in the desert, what appeared to be nothing really wasn't; the Reese River was concealed in the bottom of a wide channel that was itself hidden by the ubiquitous sagebrush. The only way to find it was to start walking east, which I did, mostly out of puzzlement. I climbed over a barbwire fence twenty yards from the road before I could see there was some kind of break ahead in the desert. It proved to be a channel about six feet deep and thirty feet across, unmarked by any greenery. The river was a shallow stream perhaps three feet wide in the bottom of the channel, happily wending its way from south to north, that probably wouldn't even qualify as a creek anywhere else. You just had to smile.

We drove north on the dirt road for several miles until it rejoined State Route 722, and followed it a short way to Highway 50. Turning east again, the highway started climbing into the foothills of the Toiyabe Mountains, between two cemeteries that were obviously still in use, although you could tell a lot of the grave markers were really old. A large stone tower—Stokes Castle—rose from a hillside above and to the south of the highway, which wound its way upward along the north side of Pony Canyon. And all of a sudden there it was: Austin.

Coming into Austin from the Reese River side felt exactly like putting on a comfortable old pair of slippers. Although I'd never seen it before, it was so familiar that the first thing that popped into my mind was, "I'm home."

Up the street on the right was Vigus's Market, marked by a sign that read "Groceries—Ice—Fishing Tackle." Fishing tackle? Thinking back to the Reese River, I chuckled. The town had a sense of humor, too.

It was hot. We parked and walked across the street to the Austin Hotel, where we had a cold brew and met Smitty, a bartender who looked and acted like a bartender and who clearly enjoyed both his job and his customers. The fact that we found that strange was a sad comment about the city life we'd become accustomed to.

We then walked up the street to Carol's Country Store and met Carol Mendenhall, who had actually done the deed: She'd sold her house in the city, quit her job, and moved to Austin. Naturally, we pummeled her with questions, paying rapt attention to the answers that reinforced our hopes and disregarding the ones that didn't.

Coincidentally, the narrow building sandwiched between her store and the Masonic Hall just happened to be for sale. The current owner, also a city transplant, had sectioned off the ground floor into small rooms fit to be leased out to miners about to move into Austin for the most recent boom, the reworking of the ore tailing piles near town to extract silver that had been missed the first time around.

We could get a really good deal now, you know? But we'd have to hurry. So we did. We signed the papers and made a down payment, the balance to be paid upon the sale of our home in the city, just that quickly, lest we miss out.

Looking back, I have no doubt that is exactly the way things have happened in Austin since the founding of the town.

The Stagecoach Inn Boarding House was only twenty-five feet wide, the common width of a lot in Austin, but it was a three-story building—remodeled from the original high-ceilinged two stories—and was long like a bowling alley. We got it for a paltry $13,000, or for what we thought of as a paltry $13,000; the locals thought it was an ungodly amount of money to pay. That's how property values eventually climb into the stratosphere, no matter the area—or the era—you're personally involved with.

There was no escrow and no title search involved, as most of the property in and around Austin was, and still is, transferred between owners by means of a quitclaim deed, which is then officially filed with the Lander County recorder. Since the seller carries the paper, leaving banks and lending institutions out of it, nothing else is needed. The overall concept of the quitclaim deed is simple, and so far it has worked fine. I would suppose, though, that if anybody ever comes up with an original, genuine title to my property, the fact that the fellow who sold it to me formally gave up any claim he had to the land, as did the inhabitant before him, probably won't give me much to take to court.

I later found that a lot of the land titles in the area were so clouded with patented mining claims and disputed surveys that you couldn't use them as collateral to borrow money, hence the widespread use of quitclaim deeds. Although there was a certain amount of anxiety over that, it did, if nothing else, keep you out of heavy debt.

We're talking 1974 dollars here, but we sold a three-bedroom, two-bath home with a double garage and built-in swimming pool, located on a corner lot in Antioch, for $35,000 in order to move to Austin. It was a good deal for us, although I felt a little guilty about fleecing the buyer, because I was positive the California market had topped out and that particular piece of property would never be worth any more than that. Ah, well, caveat emptor—"let the buyer beware," the poor slob.

However, using hindsight, it seems I ended up a little more caveat-emptored than he did. Not that it mattered, of course, because I wasn't looking to turn a profit, I was looking to get the heck out of there. Still, you know, a few bucks here, a few bucks there . . .

We pulled a twenty-four-foot U-Haul truck up to the front of the Stagecoach Inn in early July 1974. With us was half of Marlys's identical twin daughters, Kathy—at least I think it was Kathy—along with her best friend, Kelly Sloan. Having just graduated from high school the previous month, both were brimming with the adventurous spirit that goes with youth, and Austin was as much about adventure as it was anything else, even for us more adult folks.

Funny. The Stagecoach Inn looked a little older and more run-down than I remembered. And smaller, somehow. Marlys and I sat there for a few moments while it all sunk in, and then we got busy. We stayed busy too, for years. When you let go of a bird in the hand and go after one in the bush, you'll darn sure stay busy lest you start wondering, in an idle moment, what it was, exactly, that you just did.

In the short time between our buying the building and moving to Austin, the company that was to start reworking the silver tailings—for which the Stagecoach Inn had been sectioned into boardinghouse rooms—changed its mind. The boom had gone bust without a single dollar having changed hands, at least in our direction. Even as we unpacked, we were trying to figure out how to make a living without somebody, um, getting a job.

The answer came to Marlys like a bolt out of the blue; "An ice cream parlor!" she said.

"A what?" Maybe I hadn't heard right.

"An ice cream parlor," she repeated, "This is a desert. It's hot here. Why not sell ice cream?"

The enthusiasm quickly spread, in the manner of the Little Rascals when one of them would holler, "Hey, we could dress up and put on a show and charge folks a nickel!"

But really, why not?

There were a few holes in it, as things turned out, such as the desert part. Unbeknownst to us, the Great Basin Desert wasn't like the Sahara Desert or even the Mojave, as far as temperature extremes go. The Great Basin was the highest, coldest desert in North America. We would eventually find that out, but for the moment an ice cream parlor seemed not only logical, but also financially doable with the limited funds we had left.

Except for—and I got chills even thinking about it—securing the necessary permits and licenses and authorizations and inspections. Where I was from, you may as well just shoot yourself and get it over with.

I took a deep breath and walked across the street to the courthouse, where the county offices were. I stuck my head into the first doorway I came to and scoped out the enemy, then walked right in like I had every right to be there. The clerk, a young lady in a summer dress whom I later came to know as Carolyn, looked friendly enough, but I'd had my head bitten off in county offices often enough that I wasn't about to be fooled.

"Hello," she said, and then after a pause, "Aren't you the one who bought the Stagecoach Inn?"

"Yes." And here goes: "What do you need to do to open an ice cream parlor here?" I thought I'd said it too quickly, because she apparently didn't understand. She looked puzzled, and said,

"Hmm."

But after a moment's silence, she added, "Hang out a sign, I guess."

And that was that. As far as Nevada's Lander County was concerned, if you wanted to go into business, it might help to hang out a sign. The only restriction was that a county license was required for selling alcohol. I walked out thinking *Toto, we are definitely not in Kansas anymore.* (Unfortunately, that didn't last long. After the county seat was moved to Battle Mountain, our county commissioners enacted so many license requirements and codes and ordinances and fees and inspections and taxes that today you can probably open up shop in Las Vegas as easily as in Lander County. And make a lot more money than you can here, if that is the purpose of your business.)

We also checked with the state and found that we'd have to get a retail sales tax number, and that food establishments also had to be cleared by the state health department. Marlys looked into that while I stood back and looked at our building, I mean I really looked at it, with an eye to how an ice cream parlor might be made to fit in there. The new rooms on the ground floor were in the way, and there was no getting around that.

Well, the walls that had just been put in would have to come out, that's all. I got my crowbar and leaned it against the first wall. Then, because it was late July and really hot, I opened a cold brew and sat down on the doorstep to make sure I had the whole thing straight in my mind. There are those who would argue that this wasn't the best way to keep my mind straight, but I doubt they've ever built their own restaurant, at least not in Austin.

Anyway, John Nagy—a local I'd become friends with—happened by about then and joined me. Turns out John had torn out a wall or two and was giving me some pointers, while enjoying a little heat relief himself, when Harry McCoy and his wife, Linda, stopped by. Harry and Linda were hoping to move from Hawthorne to Austin, if they could find some work. Harry had never torn out a wall, but he knew a little about heat relief, so we all moved out onto the sidewalk, where there was room for a bigger ice chest and some folding chairs. We were making pretty good progress, right on the verge of actually picking up the crowbar, I think, when Frank from Sacramento drove up on his Harley and parked in front. None of us had ever met Frank, but we didn't want to be impolite, so we invited him to join us. Shortly thereafter we somehow got off track and the whole thing just turned into some kind of party or something. I do remember that we were pretty good at harmonizing.

Never having been in business for myself before, I was surprised at how it gets started. I had expected it to be more, you know, businesslike.

With John's and Harry's help we had the walls out within two days. Shortly thereafter we found a business that was offering for sale an outdated soda fountain, the kind you might see in an old W. C. Fields movie, complete with ice cream bins and carbonation equipment. In fact, this particular fountain was in a drugstore—Ramos Drugs on California Street in Reno—that was going out of business after several decades of friendly neighborhood service. We drove the 180 miles to Reno in my pickup, thought the fountain setup about the coolest thing we'd ever seen, and paid $500 for the whole kit and caboodle right on the spot.

Loading it up proved to be a bit of a problem, as the ice cream box was seven feet long, three feet high, and three feet wide, housed in stainless steel and weighing in at almost six hundred pounds all by itself. There was also a separate compressor unit—an ancient electric motor that turned a cast-iron flywheel via fan belts—that also provided hookups for the CO_2 bottles that added carbonation to ordinary tap water. To top it off there were two fountain spigots, which resembled draft beer taps, and two counter-mounted syrup dispensers labeled Coca-Cola and Hires Root Beer. They were shaped like the outboard motors that propelled the boats Dad and I used to rent to go fishing, and they would later prove to be only slightly less temperamental.

Since I was driving a half-ton Chevy pickup, I assumed that meant I could carry a half ton in the bed with no problem, but apparently that wasn't what a half-ton rating meant; not only did our load flatten the rear tires, but the bed of the pickup was compressed almost to the axle, causing the headlights to angle pointlessly up into the night sky. Luckily, we didn't get everything loaded until three o'clock in the morning, so there was little traffic on the way back to Austin, and evidently no Highway Patrol troopers at all.

We arrived in front of the Stagecoach Inn in full daylight, got a few hours of sleep, and then awoke to tackle the somewhat thorny issue of how to (1) get our massive cargo out of the truck, and (2) get it into the building.

We'd had plenty of help in Reno, along with dollies and hand trucks and even a winch. Not so here, and I was leaning against the pickup, drinking a cup of coffee and staring at the oversized bin as if I could mentally slide it out of there, when something peculiar occurred; Frank again came riding up on his Harley, returning from points east with a dozen of his husky biker buddies behind him. It took maybe an hour for them to offload all the equipment and get it inside. Just returning the hospitality, he said.

I know it sounds a bit peculiar, but these kinds of coincidences happen far more often around here, with far more precision, than can be explained. Once while driving to Fallon, I blew an engine over by Sand Mountain and found myself stalled in the middle of the travel lane with no way to get off the road and no shoulder available even if I could. The van right behind me pulled over, and the driver happened to have, in the back of his van, a portable tow bar that he'd made specifically to fit a '65 Chevy pickup; I was driving a '65 Chevy pickup. Another breakdown once left me stranded fifteen miles from the highway on a dirt road that was hidden beneath a foot of newly fallen snow. My tire tracks were the only ones coming in, and I was following them back out when my fan belt broke. It didn't seem advisable to wait for somebody to happen along on that lonely road, so although the temperature was below zero I decided to try to walk out. I had just slammed the door when I heard an engine behind me, and when I turned around here was this hay truck coming down the road. A hay truck, of all things. He gave me a ride back to town, and when I returned with my brother-in-law to get my truck a few hours later, it was obvious nobody had been over that road since the hay truck.

It's like a happy Bermuda Triangle out here.

At some point while the ice cream bin was being manhandled around, a big cast-bronze valve got broken. It was about the size of a grapefruit and had been threaded into the water line that came in at the bottom of the bin came out at the spigot stations on top. It also had a connection for the CO_2 hose. I never figured out what the purpose of the valve was, but I was pretty sure we wouldn't be making any carbonated sodas without it. Not knowing what else to do, because this thing was far older than I was and certainly not available off the shelf any more, I took it down the street to Frank Bertrand's hardware store. Frank was Austin's justice of the peace, the proprietor of Lander Lumber, and the landlord of several rental properties around town. He was compact, bespectacled, and generally looked like judges ought to look, and proprietors too. He had the most distinctive laugh I've ever heard. You could identify it from halfway across town. It sounded like a guffaw interrupted with camshaftlike exactness into equal pieces.

I showed Frank my fractured valve and asked if he had any suggestions as to what I might replace it with, or if he even knew what it was. He studied it, turning it slowly in his hands, examining the threads and the markings that were cast into it, and said: "I think I might have one."

I blinked. Say what?He walked into his lumber shed and moved some sheets of plywood away from the far wall, giving him access to an old wooden crate covered with dust. Reaching in, he moved heavy-sounding things around with much thumping amid fine clouds of dust, and came up with my valve in one hand. Not something close, or something that might work as a substitute, but the exact cast-bronze dinosaur I'd walked in with (see Bermuda Triangle, above). An old, faded tag wired to the body of the valve read $5, and that's what Frank charged me.

Holy cow. I think I may have guffawed a little myself.

With that obstacle improbably solved we horsed the rest of the equipment into place, put the compressor and CO_2 apparatus in the basement directly beneath the fountain, soldered the copper tubing we'd cut out when we moved it from its Reno home, called a refrigeration man out from Fallon to charge the thing with Freon—which cost half what the equipment did—and plugged it in. It worked. This is when, in my mind, we actually became committed to selling ice cream, so this is when we probably should have asked the state health department what was required to comply with health regulations. We didn't, though.

Instead, we built a counter around the ice cream box, leaving enough space at the end to install a doubled-basin sink, which I did even though I absolutely hate doing plumbing. Too bad, because both the sink and the countertop would have to be replaced after the state health inspector visited—the countertop because it wasn't seamless, and the sink because it wasn't NSF-approved (NSF stood for the National Sanitation Foundation, which stuck a little blue nonremovable NSF label on all equipment it approved for use in eating establishments; the sticker seemed to add quite a bit to the price). Replacing the counter wasn't a big problem, but redoing the sink was. I hate plumbing.

We also built shelves and installed a couple of cabinets behind the counter, so we could handily store dishes and glasses and things like napkin holders. It was definitely shaping up, and John and I—and Harry, when he was around—would quite often stand back and admire our work. On occasion, when the craftsmanship was especially fine, we'd toast each other with a cold brew, resulting in even more-grandiose plans for the next day. Although the plans seldom materialized, it was fun, and the locals enjoyed stopping by to chat when they saw we weren't busy. They were all appreciative of a new business coming to town, and without fail promised to be the first paying customers through the door.

We also had to install restrooms, which, because of the narrowness of the building, were necessarily small and therefore hard to work in, and . . . did I mention I hate plumbing? We were able to do most of the piping from the basement, but it was hot down there. The floors were dirt, the walls were built of stacked chunks of native granite, and the dust was kind of musty, like it had been down there a hundred years. But you could stand up without bumping your head and that was worth a little discomfort. Shoot, that was worth a lot of discomfort. (In case you're wondering, I looked the place over thoroughly before we started work. Any neat old stuff that might have been down there had long since been removed, and the same was true of the top three floors.)

We picked up some spartan metal bar stools for seating at the counter, added three four-person booths along the opposite wall, and hand-painted an Ice Cream Parlor sign, which we hung from the roof above the sidewalk. An inspection from the state health department resulted in an "A" rating, and voila! We were in business!

Um, except for the ice cream.

It was the end of August, and *hot* outside, and we hadn't really given much thought to where we'd get ice cream around here. The answer, of course, would be Fallon, 112 miles west. Carol next door made weekly runs for supplies in her refrigerated truck, but there was no freezer compartment; she used canvas containers packed with dry ice for frozen foods. Carol graciously brought in our ice cream for us until, several months later, we found a supplier who would deliver to Austin.

Another thing we noticed, just before opening the doors, was that we didn't have a cash register. I found a cigar box, filled it with change, and set it at the workstation behind the counter. Among the first customers were Billie and Walt Dory, who noticed the cigar box right off. Billie left and came back a few minutes later with an antique cash register that, she said, had been used in this very building in the 1800s. Would we like to borrow it? Wow. It was beautiful, with ornate engraving on the metal and polished wood along the sides. Billie said she no longer had the gold-weighing scales, but she pointed out the little gold-dust drawer beneath the keys. And it was entirely mechanical, with no need for electricity. It also was not equipped to print out transactions on paper tape, so we'd have to keep track manually, which didn't seem to be, and in fact wasn't, any bother. We couldn't think of anything to say but "Wow," and we did indeed borrow that cash register, for years. It became quite an attraction for customers who, like us, had never seen anything like it. Neither Billie nor Walt would ever accept anything in return, and both always said they were just glad to see it put to good use.

The ice cream parlor was small, seating a maximum of eighteen people, and took up only the first half of the ground floor. Marlys and I lived in the back, and Harry and Linda McCoy had moved into a room on the second floor so they could relocate from Hawthorne to Austin and get their boy, Robert, enrolled in school. They helped out around the place, and it was a good deal for all of us.

John lived down the street with his father and brother, Gabor and Sonny Nagy, and he was as helpful as they come. He worked at several part-time jobs around town—not at all uncommon for the Austin workforce—and prospected for gold and silver in his spare time. Without his help, at any or all hours of the day and night, I doubt we would have been able to open up while the weather was still hot, which is kind of a plus if you're selling ice cream.

And therein lay the rub. It became apparent that ice cream wasn't going to pay the bills, come winter. As the year marched into September, so did our visions of independence. Highway 50 traffic, heretofore mostly tourists, began to slack off. We'd been told to expect a slowdown of business, so it wasn't a surprise, exactly, but we were kind of surprised anyway. The locals continued their strong support, but they could eat only so much ice cream, and the chilly days were quickly approaching when comfort would dictate that they eat a whole lot less cold stuff.

We decided that we needed to expand into a full-fledged restaurant. That would mean turning our quarters in the back into a dining area and kitchen. We had the space, and we had the rudimentary knowledge of what we needed to do, but we lacked the equipment and, worse, the money to buy the equipment.

While we were batting ideas around, a Pong distributor came through, and we let him leave a machine for a split of the profits. Pong, for the information of those born later than the mid-Jurassic, was the original computer video game. A console about the size of today's ATM machines held a TV screen and two round controls, one for player A and one for player B. The screen showed only white vertical lines at each side, each line guarded by a small, white, rectangular electronic "paddle" that could be moved up and down with the dials to intercept a white electronic "ball" (actually a small white square). You wouldn't think anything that moronic would be a hit, but it was. I even thought it might get us through the winter. It didn't, though. I kept running out of quarters.

I racked my brain day and night, but it appeared that we might have miscalculated, and that somebody, in fact, might have to get some kind of job to tide us over till spring.

Rats.

ODD JOBS

anadians talk funny.

Roger owned an exploration company in Montreal that had landed a core-drilling contract around Austin, and as he and his two employees ate their ice cream, I quite frankly had a hard time understanding them. They said something about towing the rig to a drilling pad, and something about drill bits, and something about hiring a helper. I heard that last part easily enough from where I was working behind the counter. I quickly started down into the basement to check on the compressor, but it didn't do any good; Marlys heard it too, and before long I'd been hired as a driller's helper. I don't remember how much it paid, but I do remember thinking it was an awful lot of money, and it had been my experience that the more you got paid, the less you were expected to do. Since it was my sincere ambition to work myself to the very top rung of that ladder, maybe this wouldn't be so bad.

Roger shook hands and went back to Montreal. I never saw him again, but the two employees sitting at the counter with him were now my bosses.

Core drilling is a way for mining companies to get samples of underground rock with little surface disturbance and relatively little expense. It takes a crew of three: a driller, an assistant driller, and a driller's helper. If you're thinking that sounds like two chiefs to one Indian, you're on the right track.

Titles notwithstanding, though, the driller in this case was indeed a Canadian Indian who called himself Indian Ed. I never found out what his last name was, nor did I ever know the last name of his assistant driller,

Norman. Actually, we called him Norman Number Two, because Norman Number One was a driller for a different outfit that was drilling in Veatch Canyon, and neither wanted to be confused with Norman the Foreman, who was a boss for a mining company in the area at the time.

Ed was tall and thin, and Norman was a rotund French Canadian. They were like Abbot and Costello with an accent, and they ended every sentence with "eh?" whether it was a question or not. In military radio communications you let the other party know you're done talking and ready for a reply by saying "over." I figured maybe it was something like that.

Ed: "We need some oil, eh?"

Norman: "Hey"—it sounded a lot like "eh," but whenever it started a sentence, it meant they were talking to me—"grab a can of that oil over there, eh?"

Me: "Sure."

Silence. Nobody would say anything for a while, and maybe it was because they didn't know I was finished speaking. But I can tell you right now, "eh?" drove me crazy long before anything else did.

They—or we, now—were drilling in a canyon about seven miles south of town. Autumn is a great time to have an outside job because the mornings are crisp, the days are clear and often washed with a slight breeze, and you've got enough daylight to get something done but not enough to work to exhaustion. The work was really hard, and I earned every cent I was paid, which shot my wage theory all to heck. Still, it was new to me, and new jobs are always kind of enjoyable, at least until you figure out what you're doing.

Unbeknownst to me, the drilling was running behind schedule, and the enjoyment lessened somewhat when we strung lights on the tower and shifted to six fourteen-hour days per week. I thought we'd quit after the first snow—which my California brain believed was just a freak storm out here in the desert—but we didn't. We drove to work in a quarter-ton Dodge Power Wagon, one that had the "Power Wagon" logo riveted to raised ridges on each side of the hood, and that stupid thing was every bit as tough as it looked. It would get us to the drill site no matter how much it snowed.

By the time winter—a real winter, not something you'd expect in the desert at all—finally got horrible enough to keep the Canadians inside, even my bone marrow was frozen, and the happiest day of my life was the day we dismantled the drill rig and towed it out of there.

To anybody who asked, I'd allow that yes, I'd made enough money to get us through the winter, but it's a darn shame those Canadians couldn't have toughed it out till spring, eh?

Meanwhile, back at the ice cream parlor, we were now selling hot dogs and hot soup and hot chocolate, but that was about as far as we could go until we expanded into a restaurant. I spent as much of the winter as I could measuring and drawing up plans and browsing through the Reno newspapers, when we could get them, looking for used restaurant equipment.

And say, now that I wasn't working out there in it, the snow wasn't all that bad. But it sure wasn't very desertlike. Nothing says "unfair" like sagebrush bent to the ground under the weight of a foot of snow.

Spring finally did arrive, though I was beginning to have serious doubts, and the first chance I got I sat out on the bench in front, in the wonderful warm sunshine, and watched the cars go by. I hadn't been there more than five minutes when Whit Skinner, who owned Casady's Chevron station across the street, came walking over. Sometimes the locals liked to drop by and chat, so I saw no reason to run and hide.

Whit sat down beside me, smiled, and said, "You look like you could use a job."

I knew I should have run and hid.

It turned out that Whit's help, a high school student last year, was moving to Reno. I couldn't conceive of holding an outside job in Austin all through the winter months and then leaving just when the weather was getting nice, and I hinted as much to Whit: "What is he, some kind of an idiot?"

And that's how easy it is to become a service station attendant in Austin. I worked at it for a couple of weeks until Whit found another victim, and beyond that I filled in now and then throughout the summer and fall, whenever Whit got in a bind for help. Those were the last days of the full-service gas station, where the attendant filled the gas tank, cleaned the windows, checked the oil, and upon request changed wiper blades and adjusted tire pressures etc., etc. You could darn near make a career out of some cars, and when it got busy it got *busy*. I discovered I had a knack for inconsequential, banal small talk, which would serve me well later on when my position required me to mingle with politicians.

The job worked out OK for me because during slow periods I could cross the street and work on transforming the ice cream parlor into a restaurant. The tire bell at the station was so loud that when a car tripped it I could hear it even from the back of our building, and I'd come a-running. Self-serve gas stations have since made the tire bell obsolete, but on the rare occasions when I hear that *da-ding* I still get a Pavlovian urge to jump up and run across the street.

Marlys and I had moved up to the third floor of the Stagecoach Inn, and we partitioned off the ice cream parlor so we could work in the back rooms while staying open for business. When we were ready for kitchen equipment, we found a Chinese restaurant going out of business in Reno and bought nearly everything they had. That included a grill with ceiling hood, a deep fryer, a steam table, a reach-in refrigerator, a freezer, a worktable, a dish rack, and a sink, all with attached NSF labels. Delivered to our front door this time. With no sign of Frank and his sumo wrestlers to help us carry it all in, regrettably.

The trade-off for all this was that our heretofore pay-as-you-go operation was now defunct, and my odd jobs had become a necessary evil that I was going to have to endure in order have enough money to make the payments, at least until the restaurant could stand on its own.

Whether viewed as opportunity or curse, odd jobs were plentiful. Near the end of June, after sprinting across the highway in answer to the tire bell, I was confronted with a carload of geologists looking for a laborer to help them out for a week or two. They took my grimace for a smile as I "submitted my application," and they hired me on the spot. The job paid really well, but my experience with the drilling outfit had taught me that didn't necessarily mean it would be easy.

They said they were a geological survey team that measured electrical charges shot into the ground to find out what kind of minerals were there. I thought I'd just leave it at that for the time being and called Whit to tell him I had a new career, starting tomorrow, but that I should be retired from it within a week, week and a half. He said he'd try to squeak by without me.

I also told Marlys and John and Harry and Linda that I'd be unavailable to work on the kitchen for a while. They said they'd try to squeak by without me.

I was up well before daylight and unlocked the front door so the geologists could come in for coffee, implying, in effect, that if they'd like to start all the days like this, they needed to make sure a stray bolt of electricity from their gizmo didn't singe my thoughtfulness.

We drove east in the gathering light, over Austin Summit into Smoky Valley, and then south, and then took a dirt road into the middle of the valley. From there we walked maybe a half mile into the desert, pretty close, I would think, to the exact center of nowhere. I was carrying all kinds of gear, in the manner of a native bearer for Bwana, when the rim of the sun finally starting clearing the mountains. The geologists stopped and unfolded a couple of small tables and started unpacking satchels and bags and dragging out a lot of impressive-looking electronic meters and stuff. The desert was as still and quiet and clear as I'd ever seen it, and the thought that kept running through my mind was, "They're *paying* me to do this?" That's when you know life is good.

It got a little less good as the day wore on, but not much. I strung electrical wire out to contacts that were hammered into the ground, and using a hand-cranked magneto the geologists shot a current through the earth, which, they said, enabled them to map the minerals. OK by me. We did that from several different locations, all of them out in the middle of the valley, and in the following days we worked our way down nearly to Carver's Station, some sixty miles south. I never understood a single thing they said, as the song about Jeremiah's bullfrog goes, but it was a great way to pass the time. I hated to see that job end.

Things were hopping back in town, and not just with the restaurant. The construction outfit of Harker & Harker was stringing power lines in from Utah to bring store-bought electricity into Austin for the first time. Up to now, electricity was supplied by the Austin Light and Power Company, owned by the Maestretti family, via two huge diesel generators housed in the Austin Garage, which was just a stone's throw up the street from our Stagecoach Inn. The exhaust noise was muffled so well you didn't notice it above the traffic, but our building was close enough to the garage that you could feel a tremor through the sidewalk. I didn't notice how soothing it was until it wasn't there any more.

An electrical substation was built just north of Austin off Highway 305, and from there the power lines continued on west to parts unknown, at least to me. However, I was about to find out a little about it due to my next odd job, which would be scattering grass seed down the power line road.

The construction phase was completed by midsummer 1975, and shortly thereafter somebody, somewhere, decided that a fifty-mile stretch of the power line road west of Austin—from New Pass to Middlegate—was a blight that needed to be reseeded so as to blend in with the desert. Not the entire road, mind you, just fifty miles' worth.

A gentleman wearing a green hard hat walked into the ice cream parlor one afternoon and asked point blank if anybody wanted a job for the next few weeks. Shoot, I didn't even head for the basement. I was tired of working on the kitchen and even tireder of running to the gas station every time the tire bell rang. Whatever the deal was, I said tiredly, count me in.

Well, it didn't happen exactly like that, because I had to show a certain lack of enthusiasm in order to keep my reputation unsullied, but I made sure nobody butted in between me and the guy in the hard hat, and guess what? I landed the job, that's what. The wages were $8 per hour, which, although it sounds anemic today, was a lot of money in 1975. For comparison, the year before I had been making $6.35 as a journeyman maintenance welder.

The next morning, long before sunup, Paul met me at the restaurant, where we packed a couple of hungry-man lunches and filled our thermos bottles. It was on me. I figured for that kind of money I could afford to be generous, and I thought it might be good advertising for any other money-laden employers out there, especially those looking for a hard worker to scatter handfuls of seed in the desert.

We got to the job site, twenty-five miles west of Austin where the power lines crossed Highway 50, just as daylight was breaking, naturally. I was getting used to that. The construction company already had a tractor waiting there, a D-7 Caterpillar towing a set of plowing discs, and the seed was in burlap sacks in the bed of our pickup. We mixed the different kinds of seed, presumably to the finest Great Basin standards, in a tub, out of which I would fill my hopper. I'd seen these chest-carried hoppers before, in movies anyway, and they always reminded me of Johnny Appleseed. They held two or three gallons of seeds, which were then disbursed in a fan-shaped arc by means of a hand crank mounted on the side. You could adjust the amount of seed cover you were putting down by varying either the speed with which you cranked the handle or the speed with which you walked, or both. Paul spent a good hour making sure I understood, and practiced, the appropriate speeds. He said the government would be sending agents out now and then to get samples from the seeded roadway, and if it wasn't done right we'd have to go back and do it again.

Got it.

Setting the mold for the next several days, I walked up the road efficiently cranking out seeds until the hopper was empty. Then I put it down by the side of the road, walked back and got the pickup, drove to the hopper, refilled it, and started walking again. Behind me Paul disked the roadway, but he had to drag each portion twice, or three times if you count the trips back to his starting points. Whenever I thought I was too far ahead, I'd let him catch up by using my free time to explore the surrounding desert. In this manner, over the course of my employment I found an old purple whiskey bottle, two arrowheads, and a longhorn cow skull that measured forty-eight inches between horn tips. Knowing they might fall victim to Paul's disc in the event Paul went for a joyride out through the countryside, I felt it my duty to remove them to safer surroundings, and they spent the next several years on display at the Stagecoach Inn Restaurant.

Power line routes are laid out in straight lines, so they often cross mountain ranges at awkward angles, and where the ground isn't level enough for a tower it has to be bladed to form a pad, which we also seeded. Same for the roads. Wherever the terrain is too steep a road is graded out of the mountainside, but not any more road than is absolutely necessary to squeeze past.

Our particular power lines crossed both the Desatoya and Clan Alpine mountain ranges. The access roads angling through canyons and around peaks were often nothing more than broken rock piled sideways, but they had to be seeded anyway; rules are rules, after all. Still, it was a nice walk, and I tried not to dwell on my $8 an hour being translated into higher electricity rates because of the summer days I spent scattering grass seeds onto barren rock.

One such tower pad was situated on a hilltop in the Clan Alpines, accessed by a road that climbed straight up to it from the west but dropped down the other side in a series of graded switchbacks. I was seeding the bottom of the switchback road when Paul started disking the pad directly above. The pickup was parked at the base of the hill, in what would prove to be a fortunate spot beneath a granite outcropping. Paul accidentally knocked a Volkswagen-sized boulder off the hilltop, and I looked up in time to see it bounding down in great leaps, aimed right at the truck.

Uh-oh. I was unable to look away, but I did manage to hold my jaw in place with my hands. The boulder took one last, slow-motion leap toward the bull's-eye that was the cab of our transportation out of here, and smashed violently into the rock outcropping above. A piece of the outcropping ricocheted off and buckled the hood of the pickup, but the boulder itself shattered and rained down for several seconds in harmless pea-sized versions of its former self. I nearly passed out before I noticed I'd been holding my breath, and as I wobbled backward I saw Paul framed nicely by some piñon trees as he leaned over the peak of the hill, grasping his hard hat in both hands. We went home early that day.

Between mountain ranges, a Cessna 172 flew in one afternoon and landed on a dirt road intersecting the power line. It was carrying the agents Paul had spoken of, and they took cup-sized samples from the power line road, climbed back into their airplane, and flew off without so much as a how-do-you-do. Paul received a phone call that night advising him that we needed to add a bit more crested wheat seed to the mix, but otherwise everything was fine. That was the only time I ever saw anybody actually check on our work, and to tell the truth I was surprised to see that much.

Over thirty years have passed since we reseeded that road, and I go past portions of it where it crosses Highway 50 every time I drive to Fallon. For the record, it looked like a power line road the day Paul and I began seeding it, and it looks like a power line road today. One can only hope electric rates aren't too much higher because of it.

I went back to work in our about-to-be restaurant, fit and tanned and reenergized. We were finally able to add cheeseburgers and french fries to our repertoire, and as August ended we were doing a nice lunch trade in addition to ice cream. We weren't anywhere near out of the woods, but it wasn't impenetrable triple-canopy jungle anymore.

We had installed five more four-person booths in the back room and opened them for use as soon as we got everything shipshape. Marlys was cooking now, with Linda waiting tables, and as I walked back and forth finishing up miscellaneous chores in the kitchen, I'd often grab the coffee pot and top off cups on my way through the dining rooms. When I recognized a local I'd stop and chat, and sometimes have a quick cup of coffee with him or her, more because I enjoyed it than because of any business sense I might have developed.

I once noticed a repeat customer who wasn't a local, who'd been in several days in a row, and out of curiosity I asked if he was staying in town. He told me was, that he was summer help for the U.S. government and was just finishing up in this area. When I asked what he was doing, he said he counted grasshoppers. He was given a vehicle, an expense account, and a good wage, and his job was to throw a circular net backward over his shoulder into the desert, count the grasshoppers thereby ensnared, and then enter the information into a government logbook.

He wasn't kidding, and I had to wonder how that job got past me. Unfortunately I was on call for Whit's station that day, and right then the tire bell rang, so I never learned how he found the job in the first place.

By then Whit seldom used me at the station, but he did have something else in mind for me that fall: stove-oil delivery. In addition to the gas station, Whit ran the Chevron bulk plant below town. He not only carried case goods and barrels of petroleum products in the warehouse, but he also stored and distributed gasoline, diesel fuel, and stove oil from aboveground tanks.

At that time many Austin homes heated with stove oil, which was essentially diesel fuel thinned with kerosene. It was burned in stoves that used an adjustable carburetor system to drip oil into a fire pan that, ideally, sustained a steady and reliable flame as long as the oil kept coming. By mutual arrangement with Whit in one of my weakest-ever moments, I agreed that keeping the oil coming would be my duty that winter. Because the Stagecoach Inn was situated on Main Street, I hadn't spent much of my first winter driving around the back streets of Austin. Had I done so, I seriously doubt I would have agreed to drive a 400-gallon fuel truck up and down icy streets to deliver stove oil.

Some customers had regular 100-gallon or 200-gallon stove-oil tanks, which didn't require many refills over the season, but most tanks were converted 55-gallon drums, lying on their sides in cradles well above ground level so the oil would feed to the stove by gravity alone. These invariably had to be refilled at least once a month, and some more often than that. Most customers were on a "keep full" basis, which meant I had a window of a few days to fill them every month, and I could hope for nice weather in there somewhere in which to make the deliveries. A few, though, only wanted a delivery when they called and said they were about to run out, in which case I had to deliver no matter what Old Man Winter was up to.

The truck was an old World War II six-by-six with the stove-oil tank mounted where the bed used to be. If needed, all six wheels could be engaged as drive wheels, which made for pretty fair traction, and all six tires could be fitted with chains, but, man, was *that* a job. Whit demonstrated how to put the chains on, but he did it on a sunny day in September. It's a lot different when you're rolling around the snow with frozen fingers. We Californians have a tough time grasping that concept until we actually feel the coldness of snow against our skin, but by then, of course, it's too late to back out.

I delivered stove oil all winter long, and on into the modified Austin winter known as "spring." Every delivery was an education. It was hard to come to a stop going downhill by using the brakes if the road was icy, but I learned how to slide the truck sideways into a snow bank so it would stay put while I unreeled the hose and made the delivery. When the wind was howling, which was often, it would cause snowdrifts across the road that could be used in the same manner. And I didn't have to worry much about other traffic once I got off Main Street, because only an idiot would be out in that stuff.

Most of all, I learned that when the weather was nice and the roads clear was the time to deliver stove oil, even if the timing was off. Failing that, I also found I had some control over the weather; if I wanted a storm to go away and the sun to come out, all I had to do was get out there in the blizzard and chain up all six wheels.

All in all, delivering stove oil wasn't as bad as being a driller's helper, but it ran a close second on the misery scale. Thankfully, stove-oil heaters were on the way out even then, as propane and electricity offered cleaner and more efficient heating. Cost-effective woodstoves, such as Earth Stoves, also became popular in Austin, as firewood was fairly easy to get from the surrounding mountains. To the best of my recollection, stove oil had gone the way of the dodo bird by the late '70s.

The winter of '75–'76, though, showed no lessening of stove-oil deliveries, and I stuck it out to the bitter end in the sure and certain knowledge that this was not only my first winter delivering the stuff, it was also my last, no matter what.

However, Whit Skinner, bless his pointy little head, wasn't quite through with me. Had I noticed it, after I started delivering stove oil in town, I was only a nudge away from delivering fuel out of town. Whit disguised the nudge by asking if I'd like to ride out to the Monitor Ranch with him. Well, sure. What moron wouldn't? I'd never been to a Nevada ranch. Of course, we'd take them a load of diesel as long as we were going, so we'd ride out in his other delivery truck, a 1,500-gallon fuel tanker.

We left well before sunup, as Whit had loaded the truck the previous day so we could get an early start. An early start, he explained, is essential in the wintertime so you can make the delivery while dirt roads are still frozen. The weight of the fuel gives good traction on ice, but you want to get rid of it before the daily thaw starts, because that same weight will cause you to sink to the axles in mud.

"And say," he added as we started up the summit, "have you ever driven one of these split-axle transmissions?"

I saw through all this, naturally—Mom didn't raise any fools—but it took a couple of weeks, and by then I noticed I was driving the truck all by myself, delivering a load of fuel to the New Pass Mine, between stove-oil deliveries.

For reasons beyond my understanding, mines are always located near the tops of mountains, so they naturally get more snow. The owner of the mine, Don Jung, had plowed the upper part of the road, but he hadn't plowed it quite enough. The truck came to a reluctant halt, wedged solidly between two five-foot berms of plowed snow. It would go neither forward nor back, so I rolled the window down, climbed out, and walked about a mile to where Don was still at work widening the road with his tractor. Turns out I had gotten there before he was ready. In this business, not only could you start too late for your own good, you could start too early. That made me uneasy. Having to get everything just right is what got Goldilocks in trouble.

Still, most of the deliveries were to ranches, and very few of them were elevated much above valley level, so the snow out there was about the same as, or less than, we had in town, and I had a pretty good idea what to expect.

For the outlying areas I wanted to be on my way just before light started breaking in the east, naturally, which was still not my favorite part of the day. Fortunately, few people were up that early and even fewer were in a position to be run over by a fuel truck, so it worked out all right. By the time I noticed my eyes were open it was nearly daylight, and I was always surprised to find a half-full cup of lukewarm coffee in my hand. The truck would be purring along, in the right gear at the right speed, with the lights on and everything in the right position. I never hesitated to take full credit for it.

I wasn't a truck driver by trade, and I learned some things that I would rather have not learned at all. That split-axle thing, for instance; it was possible to get hung up in between somewhere, unable to put it in any gear whatever. Starting down Bob Scott Summit is not a good time to discover that. And with dual tires on the back, how do you know when one of them is flat? Answer: Four tires will only leave three tracks in the snow. Answer #2: The truck will start swaying. You won't know why, though, unless somebody tells you. Today that same truck would require a commercial driver's license to operate, and a hazardous material rating, but in those days a regular license was all that was needed. It's all about timing.

I was fortunate in that I not only survived but was able to learn where all the area ranches were in a very short time. Again, I came along near the tail end of these deliveries, because most of the fuel hauled out was diesel to keep the ranchers' electric generators running. The same store-bought electricity that had come to Austin was slowly making its way out to these very ranches. It took a couple of decades, but there were eventually no generators left to deliver fuel to.

When spring finally arrived, Whit announced he was retiring. I really hated to see him go, but on the other hand, I was plumb ecstatic to be rid of that tire bell.

Within a couple of months Joe Ramos took over the gas station, and a fellow from Ely named Brian Thomas bought the bulk plant below town. Brian got out of the stove-oil business entirely but hired me to run the rest of the bulk plant, including deliveries, on a part-time basis. And run it I did, for a while.

The Stagecoach Inn started doing very well indeed, and as soon as I could, I followed in Whit's footsteps and retired from the bulk plant business. The logical person to take over Brian's Chevron bulk plant was Joe Ramos, since he already had one of the Chevron gas stations, so that is, of course, what happened.

What amazed me most about the jobs that kept popping up around Austin was that the whole country was in the throes of high unemployment at the time, with gloom and doom all over the place.

I suspect that all small towns need more workers than are available most of the time, and if you're not picky about it, I believe anybody who wants to can go to work in places like Austin. When we moved here it seemed it should be just the opposite, that we would be lucky to survive even one year out here in the sticks if things didn't go right, but as it turned out I was offered more jobs than I could possibly accept.

The upshot of all this is, as far as jobs are concerned, I don't know how people get by in the city.

REAL JOBS

I never wanted to get another real job after I left California, because no matter how interesting a real job may be in the beginning, it always transforms itself into a tiresome chore to be done day in, day out, for as far as you can see into the future. It is this, I think, more than anything else, that caused me to move to Austin in the first place.

Odd jobs notwithstanding, after a few years the Stagecoach Inn was able to stand alone and furnish us with a fair income, but only if we gave it care and constant attention. After the construction phase, it was kind of my unfocused plan to retire in some fashion, which just didn't happen. I was always having to fix something, or add something, or change something, and because of the difficulty in keeping help I reluctantly backed into cooking. Just now and then, you understand, rather than close the place down for a day.

Somehow, a quarter of an inch at a time, cooking became my first real job in Austin. It was awful. Twelve hours standing up, tossing burgers on a hot grill and dropping french fries into boiling oil, and cleaning and mopping and doing dishes in between. And in between *that,* repairing broken things.

Out of the clear blue sky, one summer evening in 1978, Sergeant McMullin of the Lander County Sheriff's Department poked his head into the kitchen and asked if I was interested in "packing a badge." I didn't know what he meant by that, but I did know there were about ten cheeseburger orders hanging on the wheel.

"Yes!" I hollered.

These things do not, and never will, happen in cities, but Mac invited me to come by the sheriff's office the next day to discuss a career change. I was all ears.

Law enforcement in Austin has always been provided by the county sheriff, through resident deputies living in the area where they work. There's also a Nevada Highway Patrol trooper stationed there who handles traffic and can provide emergency help, but it is the deputy's responsibility to deal with crimes that occur in the area. Because politics plays such a substantial role, and because the population in the southern half of Lander County is much less than it is in the north, and because it is true that people who live in rural America are more self-sufficient and more inclined to handle things themselves, the number of deputies stationed in Austin has been recently been reduced from three full-time positions to a single deputy.

However, when I arrived, the sergeant in charge of Austin's substation and deputies was Stephen Bishop. Steve was a big fellow, about the size of TV's Hoss Cartwright, and his very presence often had a calming effect when things started getting out of hand. He wore thick Buddy Holly-type eyeglasses that seemed to accent his size, as if he needed that, and you could learn a lot about how to interact pleasantly with unpleasant people just by watching him. He would later go on to serve an elected term as sheriff of Lander County. He never sought a second term, and although I never asked why, I got the impression he wasn't a very good fit for the entrenched good ol' boy system of county politics. As it turned out, neither was I.

The first time I met Steve, I was working behind the counter of Carol's Country Store—in between odd jobs, so to speak—when he came in to buy a pack of cigarettes. I knew who he was because he was hard to miss, especially in uniform. He introduced himself as he handed me the money, and when I handed him back his change it slipped out of my hand and dropped noisily to the floor.

"Sorry," I blurted, "Cops make me nervous."

"Yeah," he replied knowingly. "Me too."

That told me all I needed to know about Sergeant Stephen Bishop.

Several deputies came and went over the next few years, including

Steve, and because we had a restaurant, we met all of them. Some I liked and some I didn't much care for, but I was surprised by the high turnover rate. Hardly any of them lasted a year, and the main reason was the one that keeps people from moving to Austin in the first place: isolation. The nearest shopping mall is in Reno, the nearest McDonald's in Fallon. Ditto for dentists and doctors, bowling alleys and drugstores, etc., etc. Apparently those things are missed by some people in direct proportion to how many months they've lived here.

For the sheriff's department the solution, naturally, was to hire somebody who'd lived here for years and train him to be a deputy. He wouldn't be going anywhere, for crying out loud. That's the way they'd hired deputies the first hundred years, and it had worked fine. However, by 1974 there was a growing body of case law suggesting that if you harbored any concerns about liability, you might want to have a law enforcement officer trained professionally *before* you pinned a badge on him, instead of the other way around.

The other reason deputies didn't last very long, although it's doubtful any of them would own up to it, is that sometimes you found yourself all alone when things started getting dicey. There was often no officer available for backup, at least not for a couple of hours. Sometimes, not very often but sometimes, the badge itself is of no help, and there is going to be physical trouble. You can get the bejeesus scared out of you in short order, and it does make you reconsider a lot of things. I know.

Because of the high turnover, there came a time in 1978, on Sergeant McMullin's watch, when the shortage was so acute it became intolerable. The newly hired deputy, in a somewhat desperate return to the practice of hiring locals, was leaving for four weeks of police training, and unless Mac could find someone to fill the third slot, he was going to have to cancel his vacation. Which is what, I believe, led him to poke his head into the kitchen and ask me if I would be interested in packing a badge.

The next morning I met with Mac at the substation, which was just up the street next to the courthouse. The building was new, having replaced the old jail in 1975. Before that, deputies hung out in an office at the courthouse, which was equipped with the most awful jail cells in existence. They're still there, as a matter of fact, and if you want to see how prisoners are kept in the substandard regions of Honduras, I imagine you'd come away with a pretty accurate idea if you took a look at those courthouse cells. It would be surprising to me if a lot of criminals didn't become preachers after a night or two in there.

Mac didn't seem troubled that I had no experience. He was a retired navy man who apparently put a lot of stock in intangibles. He flipped through the application he had me fill out and asked three questions:

"You served in the marines?"

"Yes."

"Honorable discharge?"

"Yes."

"Can you start tomorrow?"

"Yes."

Although the job was conditional upon a background check, I think it's safe to say I was probably the last working peace officer hired as offhandedly in the entire United States of America, let alone Austin.

That afternoon I put in my final shift as a fry cook, or at least my final full-time, on-purpose shift, wondering what I had gotten myself into. Being a peace officer wouldn't be like punching a time clock, though, would it? Not like a real job.

The next day Mac took me up to the judge's chambers on the second floor of the courthouse, where Judge Bertrand swore me in as . . . what, not only deputy sheriff, but deputy *coroner?* Was he kidding?

"Is he kidding?" I asked Mac.

Nope.

Now I wasn't entirely ignorant in these matters. I knew that the justice of the peace, by law, also held the office of coroner in the smaller counties, because we'd had a tourist, um, expire, in the restaurant one afternoon—it wasn't my cooking, I swear—and Judge Bertrand had convened a coroner's jury to look into it. When I brought this up, the judge smiled and informed me that the state legislature had recently directed the county sheriff take over the office of coroner, freeing the judge up for more important—and, coincidentally, more pleasant—duties. The sheriff, in turn, foisted this coroner business off on his deputies, as much as he could.

Not to fear, though. Sergeant McMullin told me he, personally, didn't expect me to pronounce anybody dead unless the body was separate from the head.

That made me feel oh so much better.

Then my journey into the law began. It took several shelves to house all the volumes of the Nevada Revised Statutes, which are intended to clearly state, to all us citizens, exactly what is legal and what is not. In practice, however, it's a murky place where you need to tread cautiously, and every time the legislature meets in Carson City the ground rules are changed, so every two years you have to recheck whatever law you're enforcing to make sure it's still there and still recognizable.

BB guns, for instance. Any idiot knows a Daisy air rifle isn't a firearm, so I never even looked it up. Shooting firearms inside town limits is illegal, unless it falls within certain exceptions such as self-defense. I ignored BB guns unless there was damage being done. For ten years I ignored them, and then I found that in Nevada a firearm was defined by the size of the projectile it shot, which was, apparently on purpose, designated by our lawmakers so that it included BB guns. My timing was good, though; shortly after it was pointed out to me, our legislators belatedly came to their vaporous senses and changed the definition of a firearm to a weapon that had something to do with combustion. Well, duh.

Although that is an extreme example of the pitfalls of law, it makes you wary. Thankfully, I wasn't aware of the BB gun lunacy until I was ready to retire and become a judge anyway.

Since I didn't know the law, and since I was expected to go out on patrol by myself and make these kinds of calls, without formal training and without the Nevada Revised Statutes at my fingertips, I asked Mac if he had any suggestions. Yes, he did: "If you see something that looks like it should be illegal, it probably is. Put a stop to it, and we'll look it up later."

That served me pretty well, except for those cussed BB guns.

Southern Lander County was, as a rule, quiet, and as such it was a good place to ease slowly into law enforcement. And even though Mac went on vacation for a few weeks and Deputy Mock was away at training, I wasn't left to founder alone. I was already friends with Rick Banovich, who was the resident Highway Patrol trooper, and the Austin dispatcher/matron was no other than Billie Dory, who'd lent us the cash register. Between the two of them I was able to familiarize myself with at least the basic stuff, such as handcuffing and radio procedures and paperwork. I rode along with Rick whenever our shifts overlapped, which was often, and while everybody else was gone he made sure he was available in case I ran into trouble.

I spent most of my shifts patrolling the back streets of town and occasionally driving out to Gillman Springs and Kingston, and around midnight I'd walk Main Street, rattling business doors to make sure they were locked, and making bar checks. I took a lot of good-natured ribbing in the bars, because there were usually friends of mine in there, among whom I used to do some partying myself. Curiously, when we were out drinking together it seemed we were all clever, and truly witty. However, as a deputy making bar checks I found my old drinking buddies to be barely amusing. It must have been my vibrant personality that spurred us to brilliance in the old days.

Not surprisingly, I found the whole business a little unsettling. The old joke "last week I couldn't even spell teecher, and now I are one" seemed to fit.

There were two sheriff's vehicles assigned to Austin: a four-wheel-drive GMC pickup and 1970 Ford Crown Victoria sedan equipped with a police package. As near as I could tell, the police package consisted of a roll bar and a beefed-up suspension to help in cornering, which did indeed help going over Austin Summit.

Like many rural Nevada sheriff's offices, we provided twenty-four-hour coverage by working twelve-hour shifts from six until six, the day shift starting at 6 AM and the night shift at 6 PM. Each of us worked six days on followed by three off, so the only time there was a gap in the coverage was when one of us went on vacation or away for training. We were paid a flat monthly salary—around $800, as I recall—so there was no overtime, although we did get extra pay for holidays. There was seldom any such thing as a forty-hour week, but all of us knew that before we hired on. Since most of my time off was spent in the restaurant anyway, I had no complaints about spending extra time at the sheriff's office and was even plumb grateful to be there at times, such as when tour buses stopped at the Stagecoach for dinner.

Full-time sheriffing didn't pay as much as any of the odd jobs I'd had, but then essential services never do, and I never met anybody who went into law enforcement for the money.

Even with the paycheck I didn't think of it as a real job, but both Marlys and I were happy to have a regular monthly income aside from the restaurant, because it made that winter much easier for our doggedly grumpy creditors, resulting in a winter that was much more pleasant for us.

Ironically, Highway 50, now officially known as "The Loneliest Road in America," may really have been the loneliest road before they put the signs up sometime in the 1980s. Before then things were better in one way, because less traffic really does equate to a better quality of life, but things were worse too, because there wasn't a lot of business to go around. Less business for a restaurateur is bad, but less business for a deputy sheriff is good, and I think I may have split my personality trying to figure out whether to mourn the lack of activity or celebrate it.

At least that's what I came to blame the breakup of my marriage to Marlys on, because it was certainly better than thinking a little thing like a metal badge could turn a nice guy like me into an officious jerk . . . nah.

At any rate, I was suddenly out of the restaurant business and living in a small house, all by myself, on the corner of Cedar and Overland streets. Marlys moved back to California, and before long the Stagecoach Inn closed for good, leaving me with an overall hangover that seemed to be shared by the town. In a few short years we'd also lost the county seat to Battle Mountain, the landmark Austin Hotel had burned to the ground, the bank was foundering, our grocery store was in trouble, and the first murder in the southern end of the county in fifty years had been reported five minutes into the start of my shift.

On the plus side, rumor had it a mine might be coming in.

As it turned out the news about a mine coming in was correct and, unfortunately, so was the report of a murder.

In a jealous fit, Jim Henson had shot and killed his wife at their residence in Gillman Springs, twenty miles southeast of Austin in Smoky Valley. A lieutenant's slot had replaced the sergeant's position, in order that the Austin commander would have administrative authority to run the entire substation, with Jack Emery filling that slot at the time. I would be the investigating officer, so I had to take somebody else to act as coroner, and Jack was forever grateful that I stopped by and got him. Henson had driven into town to report the death of his wife, by suicide, so we took him with us in the back of the squad car.

The Nevada Division of Investigations, realizing that major crimes in rural counties were often mishandled because local law enforcement agencies didn't have the manpower, the training, or the equipment to investigate properly, had several agents and a crime scene van available to come out and process just this sort of thing. Nobody in Lander County, including Lt. Emery, myself, or the sheriff, was aware of that. For the first two weeks we handled it ourselves.

We found Peggy Henson lying faceup on the living room carpet, with a Charter Arms revolver lying loosely in her open right hand. The whole thing looked wrong, even to me. Before we touched anything I offhandedly took two rolls of Polaroid pictures. For purposes of officially recording the crime scene as it was when we arrived, though, I took several rolls of 35 mm photos with our professional crime-scene camera, which was kept in an aluminum case in the trunk of the patrol car. This would be the starting point of the case should it ever end up in court. I'd never used the 35 mm before, but how hard could it be? Well, harder than I thought; none of the 35 mm pictures I took that day turned out, and all we had to take into court were the Polaroids.

After we finished, we had the Austin ambulance come out and transport the body to town, where it was picked up by a funeral home and taken to the Washoe County crime lab for autopsy. We then sealed the house and applied to the court for a search warrant.

Jim Henson, meanwhile, seemed so darned sincere that neither Jack nor I thought he had done it. However, Jack—having been through something like this years before in Eureka County—asked for and got Jim to agree to both a paraffin test of his hands and a lie detector test. The paraffin test was designed to check for phosphates, which might be indicative of having fired a gun. We couldn't do it in Austin, but Jack found that the Fallon Police Department, 112 miles west, had that capability, so we placed paper sacks over Jim's hands to preserve whatever evidence might be on them, and I drove him in. The paraffin test, as it turned out, was a long-dead dinosaur. With a snicker or two, the corporal to whom I was directed walked me through the procedure of taking swabs for "atomic absorption," which was a much more reliable test, from both of Jim's hands. The swabs were then shipped to the FBI lab in Quantico, Virginia, for analysis. The results eventually came back positive, meaning Henson had fired a gun.

The lie detector test was performed in our office in Austin. The operator came up with a set of questions after talking with Jack and me, and when he asked if we thought Henson did it, we told him that no, he obviously didn't, but we wanted to cover all bases. When the operator was finished he came back and assured us that Jim Henson did not, in fact, shoot his wife.

With a search warrant in hand, Jack and I returned to Henson's place two days later and loaded up everything that even remotely looked like it might be evidence. That included some sheets of plywood from the back of the house that were spattered with drops of something red, which would turn out to be redwood stain, and the Henson flatbed truck. The truck had some dried red stains on the floorboard that later proved to be residue from spilled hydraulic fluid, but how were we to know? We found enough evidence of this sort to fill the entire bed of the truck, and we had the whole shebang towed to the crime lab. To keep the chain of evidence intact, I had to drive along behind, never letting the truck out of my sight. The sergeant from the crime lab took one look at the mountainous load of might-be evidence and said, "Why didn't you have the NDI mobile lab come out and test this stuff in place?"

The what?

I relayed his suggestion to Jack, who looked into it, and sure enough, we could have saved ourselves a whole lot of trouble. From that point on, though, the Nevada Division of Investigation did send their agents out to assist us whenever we needed it, which was a major help indeed.

Because I was the initial investigator, I was also required to attend the autopsy of Peggy Henson so I could take into custody any evidence that might be found. I had a really, really hard time watching the first autopsy I'd ever seen, and I had to step outside a couple of times when I got exceptionally woozy. I did take into evidence a fragmented bullet that was found lodged in her head.

As the investigation went on, it began to look like Jim Henson might indeed have done it, so Jack got him to agree to another lie detector test. We told the operator beforehand that now we just didn't know if Henson was involved or not. The test, exactly the same as the first, came back inconclusive this time. We raised our collective eyebrows at that one. A full two months after the murder, the case finally broke when Henson, apparently becoming impatient with the glacial pace of the investigation, reported several valuables missing from his residence. He said he must have been too upset to have noticed, but that the killer no doubt took the missing items the night he shot Peggy. No doubt.

One of the items was a valuable and unique sterling silverware set. Unfortunately for Henson, the friend with whom he entrusted the silverware set called us and said Henson had left it with him and told him to hide it—that he needed to "throw the cops off." We finally had Jim Henson dead to rights, although he still denied it. He took yet another lie detector test, after we told the operator of our new, airtight, evidence. This test came back positive, and the operator said he was certain Jim was the killer. At that point I couldn't help myself, and I asked the operator, who was the same one who'd administered the first two tests, how that could possibly be, how the same questions asked of the same man about the same incident could possibly result in three such contradictory conclusions. He shrugged and said, "It happens." Had I not seen and heard that for myself I wouldn't have believed it. I finally understood why lie detector results weren't admissible in court, and it's still inconceivable to me that employers are allowed to determine their employees' fitness on the basis of lie detector tests. Ouija boards are just as accurate, maybe more so.

Lie detectors notwithstanding, investigations of this sort—which is to say, mildly blundering—were common in rural Nevada counties before NDI put together their mobile crime lab. We got a conviction on Jim Henson from a twelve-person jury in Battle Mountain, but if the right questions had been asked by the defense attorney there's no doubt in my mind he would have gone free. We had other major crimes in the area before I retired, but thanks to Henson we always called NDI to process the crime scene.

During this time, both Austin and Kingston were booming. The Victorine Mine and Brazos Mill brought a sagebrush version of urban sprawl to the mouth of Kingston Canyon, and Austin Resources had opened its mill on the northern edge of town. In addition, Austin Gold Venture had started preliminary work on the road from their future mill site, seven miles south of Austin, to the mine at the top of the Toiyabe Mountains above Dry Canyon. Miners and construction workers, some with families and some without, were moving in left and right. Things were happening way too fast to suit me, which, frankly, didn't take much.

A fourth deputy was assigned to Austin because of the sudden growth we were experiencing, and we signed up five reserve deputies to help us on an as-needed basis. As it turned out, we needed them pretty often. When Jack Emery retired, I accepted the lieutenant's position, but I really didn't want it. I should have listened to my better judgment; the lieutenant's bars somehow made it a real job, and due to burn-out I resigned in the summer of '85.

Upon becoming a gentleman of leisure I found my station in life right away, on top of the redwood picnic table in my front yard. I'd take a pillow out there and lie on my back, watching the summer clouds for pirate ships and dragons. The problem was, people kept stopping by and offering me jobs. It was worse than my early days in the restaurant, and I finally accepted a part-time job delivering mail up Reese River Valley just to keep from being pestered. I sure hated to leave that picnic table.

In really rural areas, mail is delivered to outlying areas by private contractors. They aren't employees of the U.S. Postal Service, and they have to furnish everything they need to get the job done, from vehicles to tire chains. Routes are awarded to contractors who submit the lowest sealed bid and meet USPS standards. If you've ever addressed a letter to a box number that is preceded by HC—short for Highway Contract, as in HC60, Box 100—you've sent it by private contractor out of the hometown post office. These used to be called Star Routes, which I thought had a nicer ring to it, but time marches on out in the sticks, too.

Mike McGuinness had recently won the bid for the Reese River mail contract, upon the retirement of longtime mail carriers Reese and Elisa Gandolfo, but he was moving from Austin and needed someone to run the route for him. On weekday mornings, the route ran some twenty-five miles west to the Campbell Creek Ranch. On Monday, Wednesday, and Friday afternoons, however, the mail was taken up Reese River as far as the Yomba Shoshone Indian Reservation, then over the Shoshone Mountains to the settlement of Ione, and finally down Ione Valley to the mailbox at Berlin-Ichthyosaur State Park. It was sixty miles of mostly dirt road through both desert and mountains, and I loved the drive from the very start. So for the next couple of years, five days a week, that's what I did. It was enjoyable, at least during nice weather, but I gotta admit, it took a long time to get over that picnic table.

The Reese River mail route has always been known simply as "the stage," as in "Hey, I hear you're driving the stage these days," and perhaps the familiarity inherent in that was one of the reasons the route itself was so informal. There was a grocery store in Ione back then, and it wasn't uncommon to find shopping lists wrapped around money in the mailboxes at the Indian reservation. It was never very much of a list, probably because you can't fit many groceries into a mailbox, but I'd stop at the store whenever that happened and drop the groceries and change off on my way back through the reservation. In return I found snacks waiting for me in the mailboxes now and then, which I thought was a darn good trade.

On other fronts, I first met Valerie Gandolfo when she was a relief dispatcher at the sheriff's office. She was an Austin native, and we got along so well we finally married in 1986. When I found we were going to have a daughter, I spent a lot of mail route hours racking my noodle for a name. It had to be original. It had to have meaning. It had to have the ring of greatness. Let's see, um . . . the idea hit with such force that it caused me to swerve off the road . . . Withanee! My personal mail was forever incorrectly addressed to Anderson, but her first name would explain how to spell her last name, Andersen, With an "e," so, in theory at least, she'd never have to put up with that annoyance.

Val looked at me that evening. Withanee? After a while she slowly nodded.

"I like it," she said.

We had to get a bigger house, for sure. And the mail route would have to go, in order for me to get a job that paid enough to make house payments. Ah, well. Perhaps we could get a picnic table some other day. My sister and her husband, Jim and Jean Hardin, visited every year from their home in Oregon, and they bought my house on Cedar and Overland streets to use as a summer cabin. In turn, Val and I bought a double-wide mobile home to put on her lots, which overlooked the Reese River Valley, and we were set. Val's boys, Josh and Jed, got their own rooms at last, and so did Withanee.

What I got was another real job, darn it, this time as a security guard at the newly built Austin Gold Venture mill at the mouth of Dry Canyon. Val finally received her degree from BYU in Utah and took a teaching job in Austin's school, where she had been working as a teacher's aide and bus driver, so what she got was a real job, too. Nyah-nyah.

Private security guards are normally not law enforcement officers and have no inherent police powers. Their authority, as regards detaining people and conducting searches, is given them by their employer, and their jurisdiction is limited to company property. Citizens of the United States have the power to make a citizen's arrest and turn the violator over to law enforcement, which gives all of us, including security guards, the power of arrest under certain circumstances. The thing security guards have to be sure of is that the person they're arresting has broken a state law and not merely violated company policy. The only way we were different from other Gold Venture employees was that we wore blue uniforms and green hard hats.

We usually just sat in a tiny office at the gate and recorded the names and times of people entering and leaving. We worked what amounted to four twelve-hour shifts per week on rotating shifts, but the schedule was so convoluted that we somehow ended up with exactly forty hours a week. Haul-paks, those huge yellow trucks you sometimes see on the National Geographic channel, brought ore down to the mill from the mine pit on top of the mountain, but they didn't work on weekends. Since the mill did, whatever guard was working was supposed to drive up to the pit at night and make sure everything was secure. The switchback road to the top, once barely passable for a cautious and usually terrified driver, had been widened to perhaps thirty feet and was protected by a four-foot-high berm on the valley side. There were no lights anywhere on the weekend—even the mine pit generators were shut down—and I suppose it could get spooky up there, if you were predisposed to spookiness.

One of the switchbacks held unpleasant memories for me, because a few years before it had been the point at which we left the road and four-wheeled up the mountainside to get as close as possible to the site of a plane crash. We had to bring out the bodies of the pilot and two passengers, and things like that stay with me a long time. The switchback always brought back those uninvited memories, and I was driving down from the mine around midnight one weekend, in a rare heavy, swirling fog, when my headlights swept around that ominous switchback and illuminated some vertical strands of fog that for a moment, just for a moment, mind you, resembled three tattered, malformed bodies standing there. I had no trouble staying awake the rest of that shift, or indeed the rest of that week.

I often stopped and got out of my car on the very crest of the Toiyabe Mountains. On a moonlit night you could get an inspiring view of the Reese River Valley far below and the mountain ranges beyond. When there was no moon, the night was so black you could only tell where the sky ended by the absence of stars below the horizon. I was always surprised to hear crickets up there, so far above the tree line.

While standing on the mountaintop one moonless night in October, I witnessed the fiery reentry of a Russian satellite. It burned as intensely as white phosphorus, lighting up the whole valley as bright as daylight. As it streaked across the sky from south to north it was obviously breaking up, shredding miniature fireballs, and although it looked like it was right over the valley, in fact it was over the California coast. I read later that a piece of it landed in a motel parking lot in Santa Rosa. A man of lesser composure that night might have believed he was seeing an Alien Mother Ship dropping off little flying saucers as it went. Of course that never occurred to me, but as soon as my hair relaxed enough to allow my hard hat to resettle on my head, I was out of there.

I hadn't worked there very long when the price of gold plummeted and Austin Gold Venture began its slow fade into history. At about the same time, the postal service was restructuring the mail routing system, resulting in a new highway contract to be bid out of the Austin post office. The route would run Monday through Saturday from Austin to Kingston and back, a round trip of sixty miles. Val submitted a bid, and darned if we didn't get it. Real job #4, though on a lesser scale.

There were three things wrong with it. The first was that it traversed both Austin and Bob Scott summits, which made it a real pain in the neck in winter months. The second was that the entire route was paved, so there was road construction in two of the four years we ran it, which made it a real pain in the neck in summer. The third was that Smoky Valley is one of the most consistently windy places I've ever seen, which made handling little pieces of mail a real pain in the neck all of the time.

Well, there were four things wrong with it if you count the pay. We hadn't bid high enough to support our growing daughter in the luxury to which I'd become accustomed. Therefore, when Undersheriff Frank Hobbs offered me another shot at a deputy's position with the guarantee I'd never suffer promotion, I grabbed it. We still had two years left on the mail contract, so Frank said I could work the night shift if I wished, which would leave me free to run the mail during the day.

How good could it get? I now had *two* real jobs, and I would have them for *two* real years.

My wife's sister and her husband, Michelle and Robbie Quertermous, lived right below us, and Robbie agreed to run the mail for me on days I was tied up on sheriff's stuff. I'd worked with Robbie at Austin Gold Venture, and he'd stuck with it throughout the reclamation work after the mill shut down, but he was now essentially a man of leisure. Although we were good friends, there was no doubt in my mind that he was the type who'd be out loafing on a picnic table, given half a chance. It was fun to put a guy like that to work.

I had him take the mail run the morning Billie dispatched me to assist Deputy Mike True out in Kingston. It appeared southern Lander County had just experienced its second murder in the past sixty years. She had already called for NDI to come out, but in the meantime there were coroner duties to be attended to.

Bill Rhinehart, the shooter, was a sickly older fellow who lived in a converted bread van on some land right at the mouth of Kingston Canyon. Although that sounds pretty lowbrow, he'd done a lot of rockwork out there, stacking the plentiful flat shale into curving and very pleasing walls, columns, and fountains. He didn't use mortar, and must have figured out how the old-timers stacked rock so the final structure had inherent strength without using anything to hold it together. I'd known Bill for years, and when he claimed to have been a welder on NASA projects, I believed him. I was a welder by trade, and in talking with Bill it was apparent he'd forgotten more about welding than I ever knew. Trouble was, as my uncle would have put it, "the bottle got him." NASA notwithstanding, when I was around Bill I had the feeling that he'd slipped out of his time, that his personality might have better fit into the last century. He just didn't seem to belong here.

The victim was a young man named Jim Peterson, a miner whose body we found lying facedown on the floor of Bill's van. Bill claimed he'd shot Peterson in self-defense, which, from the bruises and cuts on Bill's face, was probably true. However, I counted seven bullet holes in the victim without even moving him, and there comes a point when self-defense is no longer relevant, such as when the assailant is incapacitated. Bill said if there were seven bullet holes in Peterson, then he must have "missed a few times." He said he'd emptied his .44 revolver into the victim twice, having paused to reload it, and then used a .30-30 rifle to finish him off.

Holy cow.

The case dragged on for a couple of years without ever going to trial, and it was my understanding that Bill finally pled guilty to a gross misdemeanor, which would be far less serious than even manslaughter, just before he passed away.

The mines were soon a distant memory, and Austin had mellowed out again, which is the way I liked it. In police work my favorite saying was "Bored is good," and I meant it. But police work was also changing. No longer could we throw prisoners in jail and then lock up the office and go home, leaving a note for the day shift. Prisoners had to have twenty-four-hour jailers now, in case they needed a snack, I guess, so our jail became nothing more than holding cells for prisoners being taken through or waiting to appear in court next door.

On top of that, the Lander County jail in Battle Mountain had been condemned by the state, so we couldn't take prisoners there either. Eureka County had the nearest facility, seventy miles east, so if we needed to lock somebody up overnight we had to haul them over there.

More disturbing was the nitpicky little stuff. The sheriff's department had become unionized, which meant collective bargaining steered our fates and dictated what we could and could not do and what, exactly, we would receive in exchange. Now we had overtime and standby time and call time, and every minute of our duty time had to be accounted for on paper lest something end up in court or, worse, arbitration.

I hated to quit, because there was still a lot about it that I enjoyed, but for the most part sheriffing had again turned into a real job for me, lacking only the time clock.

As fate would have it, right about then Judge Bertrand announced his retirement. After twenty-seven years he'd become a fixture in the courthouse, and it was difficult to imagine somebody else sitting in his chambers, running his courtroom. I'd served as his bailiff on many occasions when I wasn't testifying as a witness. I was used to Judge Bertrand, darn it, and all these changes were getting a bit overwhelming. My wife suggested that the sensible thing to do would be to run for judge myself.

The official title is Justice of the Peace, and by Nevada law there has to be one such position for every thirty-five thousand citizens. You get away from Las Vegas and Reno though, and the population drops below that for most entire rural counties, so many justice courts exist because the areas they serve are so far away from population centers. Lander County, with a total population of under eight thousand, has two townships a hundred miles apart, each administered by a local justice court. Because the caseload is usually small in these courts, so is the judge's salary, and for that reason the judges aren't required to be attorneys or, in fact, have any legal training whatever. When Judge Bertrand started his career, he did so all by himself. You know, just don the robe and hear the case. Fortunately, since then the National Judicial College—the only such school in the nation— opened its doors in 1963 from, of all places, the campus of the University of Nevada in Reno, 176 miles west of Austin. Nonattorney judges from all over the United States are now able, and in many cases required, to undergo two weeks of training at the college before hearing their first case. Whether you are the new judge or the new litigant, whew; guinea pigs are no longer necessary, thank you.

First, though, came the election. Austin Township, for purposes of the office of justice of the peace, consisted of the southern half of Lander County. You had to live there in order to file for judge, but there were few requirements beyond that, and a total of eight of us threw our hats into the ring. We all knew each other, and we all knew the voters, and the voters knew all of us, so there really wasn't a need for the kind of campaigns you see in the city. Oh, we posted signs and handed out pens and hats and buttons, and we spoke at the obligatory candidates' night held at the town hall, but I'm not sure any of it was necessary. It seemed to be widely held that it would come down to the current court clerk and myself by the time of the general election, and that was exactly what happened. In my mind the general election could have gone either way, but I ended up the new JP—short for justice of the peace, in the jargon of us adjudicators.

After being sworn in by the district judge in Battle Mountain, I moved into the judge's chambers on the second floor of the courthouse. When Austin was still the county seat, the judge's chambers and the courtroom were the province of the district judge. Austin's justice of the peace was allowed to use the courtroom when it wasn't in use by the district court, and nothing more. That changed with the county seat transfer, when all of a sudden the justice of the peace of Austin Township owned the courtroom, the judge's chambers, and the court clerk's office. There wasn't much benefit to losing the county seat, but there was that one silver lining.

This is the court I inherited when I took office, and for all the years I worked there I never once lost the sense of awe evoked by the polished wood and the antique furniture and the high ceilings. In Judicial College I'd been introduced to the phrase "the majesty of the court," which refers to the trappings—the robes and the high-backed chairs and the gavels and flagstaffs and seals and all the other accessories—that were intended to set the courts apart from any other agency, and to instill a sense of respect and reverence. Austin's courtroom had a majesty all its own, given it by the builders who crafted it, so I always felt we had a head start in that category.

I was the only thing that didn't seem to fit. While my police work had made me familiar with laws when it came to criminal cases, concepts such as hearsay and the admission of evidence were argued back and forth in the courtroom by attorneys who, I suspected, weren't as interested in the truth as they were in presenting their side in a favorable light. The courses I had attended on these subjects were necessarily brief and covered only content, not passion. My rulings on these vague and wispy concepts were therefore shaky, and not nearly as clear as I would have liked. The difficulty is that it takes time to be able to tell the wheat from the chaff, and all the education in the world is no substitute for actually sitting on the bench.

Small-claims cases, on the other hand, exposed a problem that every small-town judge comes up against: everybody knows everybody else. I knew the parties and the parties knew each other, and the most difficult part was at the very beginning, because we had to cease being Joe, Fred, and Jim and become plaintiff and defendant and judge. Once that was done (and there were times when it was a real chore), the hearing usually smoothed out to where facts could be presented calmly, at least on the surface.

Thank heavens not very many of these cases made it to court, and the credit in most cases can be given, even today, to Judge Frank Bertrand. Frank realized that civil lawsuits between erstwhile friends in small towns always caused problems later on, no matter who won. The very act of going to court made rifts between townspeople who took one side or the other, and occasionally divided the entire community. Frank thought if he could keep a dispute from developing into an official hearing in a courtroom, which causes every real and imagined grievance to be forever burned into the psyche of everyone involved, the resulting settlement wouldn't be as painful, or as lasting. So Frank came up with what he called a courtesy letter; before a claim was filed with the court he sent out a letter to the defendant, on official court stationery, describing the problem and suggesting that if there were anything to the claim the defendant might want to take care of it before it went any further, to avoid having to pay additional court costs. The letter also explained that if the defendant felt he didn't owe the money, to please disregard the enclosed information and prepare for the hearing.

This simple little letter worked wonders, which I knew from personal experience. Several years before, I had been on the receiving end of one after I bought some used restaurant equipment that I was slow in paying for because I didn't like the way I'd been treated by the guy who sold it to me. However, when I received that letter from the court, it dawned on me that I had stuff that I hadn't paid for, no matter the circumstances, and going to court over it would not only be incredibly dumb, it would be futile and expensive. I made arrangements to pay my debt, and then I walked over to the courthouse and personally thanked Frank. If you know you're wrong, it doesn't take a big push to open your eyes.

Two-thirds of all small claims that came into Austin Justice Court were settled by means of this courtesy letter before anything official took place. That is an incredible number, and if transposed to all the justice courts in the state it would greatly reduce the number of civil filings, which are said to be clogging the system. However, it also greatly reduces the statistics for each individual court, which are used to justify the budgets, and the salaries, and even the continued existence of some smaller courts. I was disheartened when other judges around the state pointed that out to me and opted not to use the courtesy letter for that reason. I had a hard time listening to judges whine about their horrible caseloads after that, though.

Being the judge in a small community raises your stature, whether you deserve it or not, and whether you want it or not. Whenever I was introduced, tacked on the very end was, "He's the judge." I had to keep remembering that. Because I'd been a deputy sheriff I was aware that those in authority are constantly on display, so it shouldn't have come as a surprise, but in a manner of speaking it did. The difference was that by law justice courts never close, and therefore a justice of the peace is never, ever, "off." He goes on duty when he's sworn in and goes off duty at the end of his elected term, which is six years. I'd never gone six years without a day off. Unthinkable as it was, I would end up stretching that to twelve years.

Judges have a tendency to stick around for a long time, as evidenced by the fact that I was only the twelfth justice of the peace to ever hold office in Austin. That told me the position must be either (1) immensely satisfying, or (2) ridiculously easy. Well, the answer is both. And neither. But I *was* being addressed as "Your Honor." Since it had taken me fifty years to become respectable, I thought I might like to hang on to it for a while.

Near the end of my first term in Austin, I was offered the position of tribal judge of the Yomba Shoshone Tribal Court, which was located on the Indian reservation forty-five miles south of Austin in Reese River Valley. I'd been through there a couple hundred times while carrying the mail and had always enjoyed the drive, so I signed a one-year contract in which I agreed to hold court on the reservation one day a month. There were no trappings to invoke "the majesty of the court" out there, as court hearings were held in a regular meeting room around a regular table with everyone seated in regular chairs. I wore a suit and tie and sat up as straight as I could, and because the tribe treated it as a genuine court presided over by a genuine judge, it worked out just fine. I never once had to remind anybody to take off their hat or quit chewing gum, and the respect shown was seldom less than I saw in Austin.

The laws followed by state courts, including Austin's, are compiled in sixty-three loose-leaf volumes of Nevada Revised Statutes that, as the name implies, are revised and invariably expanded whenever our state legislature meets, which is in odd-numbered years. In contrast, the laws followed by the Yomba Shoshone Tribal Court are compiled in one volume of the Tribal Law and Order Code, which is revised by the tribal council whenever there is a pressing need to do so. Surprisingly, most everything that needs addressing is addressed in that one volume. Makes you wonder, doesn't it?

As I write this, I'm starting my twelfth and final year as Austin justice of the peace, and I'm also starting my seventh year as Yomba tribal judge. The tribal position may well turn out to be the last real job I'll ever hold, unless you count retirement, of course, and that's one time clock I don't mind punching at all.

SOCIALLY SPEAKING

The premier question you get asked if you live in Austin is, "What do you *do* here?" The inflection, along with the wording, strongly suggests we probably don't do anything of interest, and very little of worth. The second part, often left unsaid, is, "I mean, like, there's no *mall!!*"

True, but there's one in Reno if we really need it.

Had I been asked what I did in California, I could have answered quickly; "I'm a maintenance welder. I punch a time clock at a paper mill, when I'm not running up a bar tab at the Little Corral Saloon." Succinct. To the point. And as exciting as a Tupperware party.

I can say this: If I have dull moments now, they are of my own making. And frankly, I don't mind making a lot of them these days.

I didn't feel like that when I first moved here, though, and it was clear from the beginning that Austin was awash with opportunities you just don't have in big cities. What do we do here? Well, for starters we can join the fire department.

Most small towns rely on volunteer fire departments instead of highly paid professional firefighters, for obvious reasons. Volunteer departments are usually undermanned and welcome new members with open arms, although I certainly wasn't aware of it at the time. I knew that the fire station was across the street from our new old building, because a sign said so, but I was too busy to really notice it.

One night while I was sound asleep in the Stagecoach Inn, I was woken by a piercing wail splitting the night. *Air raid siren!!* (I grew up during the cold war, stupid. But usually not this stupid.) Startled out of my wits and lacking an air raid shelter, I jumped up and ran face-first into a brick wall that wasn't there in my former life.

Turns out it wasn't an air raid, though; it was a fire. There were two civil defense–type sirens hooked into Austin's fire warning system: one on the roof of the courthouse and one on the water tower above Sixth Street. They were activated by pulling a handle on any of the red fire alarm boxes mounted on power poles around town. A corresponding light would then blink on the master board displayed in the firehouse, showing the location of the tripped box and therefore, theoretically, the fire. It worked surprisingly well.

On this particular night I had a front row seat to the activity at the firehouse. I sat at the street window, holding an ice pack to my nose in hopes of checking the swelling, and watched a half dozen cars and pickups come roaring up at almost the same instant. This was my first look at volunteer firemen responding to a call, and it was riveting, let me tell you. There was much locking of wheels and skidding, followed by a bevy of slamming doors and shadowy figures racing into the side door of the fire station. The front door started rolling up, allowing a growing wedge of light to spill out onto Main Street, and somebody mercifully shut off the siren. When the truck rolled out, punctuated by a single red rotating beacon atop the cab, I was impressed. It was a real fire truck, with gold leaf lettering on the doors and chrome fittings glittering along the side. The bed was full of layered yellow fire hose, and the back step supported four helmeted and booted firemen, one hanging on with one hand while still shrugging into his turn-out coat with the other.

A short time later I joined the fire department and, to my surprise, immediately landed the much sought-after position of secretary. Looked like I was fireman material, all right.

Meetings were held at the firehouse twice a month on Wednesday evenings, and the new fire chief, Joe Ramos, thought it would be beneficial to signal the meetings by sounding the fire siren. This would accomplish two things: First, by tripping the siren from a different box each time, he could make sure, eventually, that they all worked. The second thing was that none of us could use the excuse that we "forgot" about the meeting. A third benefit, as it turned out, was that the townspeople got somewhat used to the siren, at least to the point where it wouldn't cause them—or us—to jump out of our respective skins when it sounded.

Further, because we were aware that all work and no play is what killed the cat, we opened the office bar after meetings, and in time outfitted the meeting room with a pool table and shuffleboard—you know, to keep the interest up. This is where the social part came in, but it didn't end there; traditionally, the fire department also hosted the annual New Year's Eve and Fourth of July dances, colored Easter eggs at the firehouse prior to presiding over Austin's Easter egg hunt at the rodeo grounds, and conducted turkey shoots in the spring and fall.

Turkey shoots? Old movies provided me with the only information I had on turkey shoots. Davy Crockett would sight down his flintlock rifle while making a gobbling noise, and when the turkey foolishly poked his head up, Davy would pop him.

I had no idea people still held turkey shoots, until we—as in members of the fire department—voted to have one. Since I was the new member, Chief Ramos asked me point-blank if I could pick up the turkeys in Fallon.

Well, gosh, um, how many?

"Three dozen," he said.

HOLY COW!! My mind shorted out, and I was unable to picture thirty-six strutting, gobbling turkeys somehow penned in the bed of my pickup. Turkeys are awful big birds, you know? And noisy, if the movies have it right. And what was I supposed to do with them when I got back? Put them in the firehouse? And what do you feed them, little bales of turkey hay?

The questions welled up so fast and furious they created a mental logjam that kept me from blurting anything out, thank goodness, because it soon come to light they were talking about frozen turkeys. Oh, *frozen* turkeys! I felt almost giddy, because I'd come within a razor's width of making a complete and everlasting fool of myself. Whew. But if they're frozen, er . . .

"You shoot at frozen turkeys?" I blurted out.

Well, of course not, but with that question I pretty well torpedoed any chance I had to blend in for the next few years.

What the contestants shot at were paper plates stapled to posts at measured distances. Each shooter got one plate and one shot, and whoever was closest to center won the turkey. There was also trapshooting, where shot-gunners fired at clay pigeons thrown out and away from them by a spring-loaded thrower.

All in all they are wonderful gatherings, with shooters and their families coming from all over Nevada, but Davy Crockett had gotten it all wrong; turkey shoots have almost nothing to do with turkeys.

I didn't last very long as a volunteer fireman, and one reason is that Marlys and I had moved to the third floor of the Stagecoach Inn. The trouble I had was that in the middle of the night, when most fires seem to strike, I'm not the most together person you ever saw. Sometimes I'm not wide awake even when I'm wide awake, and negotiating two flights of stairs in the dark, while trying to pull my shirt on, with a blaring siren pushing me along, was probably not the most judicious use of my time here on earth. To add to the perils, my timing was such that I went running across the highway about the same time as the cars, driven by adrenaline-charged responders, were arriving. My focus was so locked on the firehouse that at times I fairly bounded between them, like a deer with shirttails, and the chief admonished me more than once to be careful. I assured him I would, and I meant it too, because after crossing the street I *was* awake.

The fire department somehow staggered along without me after I quit, and is still alive and well. The siren was replaced with a pager system, so no one is blasted awake anymore when there's a fire in the middle of the night. And the volunteers just keep volunteering, may God bless them.

About the time I retired from firefighting, another community service group was forming. Ray Salisbury, who owned the local wrecking yard, was putting together the Lander County Search and Rescue team, with the blessings of both the sheriff and the fire department. Before GPS and cell phones, it wasn't all that hard to get lost in central Nevada, and the new unit seemed a worthwhile effort. So I joined up. The only actual operation I was involved in was the rescue of Hank.

Hank fell into a sixty-foot mine shaft situated at the top of "A" hill. His owner knew he was down there because he could hear Hank barking, but he couldn't find any way to get him out. The shaft was maybe fifteen degrees from vertical, which made it practically inaccessible.

So we were activated. I was told to get to the top of "A" hill in a hurry, as Hank had fallen into a mine shaft. My heart was in my throat as I drove up to the knot of cars and people at the crest of the hill. I couldn't for the life of me place Hank, but I'd been in Austin long enough that I was sure I must know him, or his family. I wasn't at all sure I was up to this.

They were looking for someone to lower down on the end of a rope when I got there, and I was so relieved to find out Hank was a dog that it just popped out: "I'll go," I said with a big happy smile.

I was given a hard hat and a pair of gloves while our knot expert tied a rope—which was first threaded through a length of plastic pipe to keep it from chaffing on the rock—around my waist. As my fellow teammates lowered, I leaned back against the rope and sort of walked down. I could hear Hank down there growling, probably scared out of his wits. The plan was to secure Hank in a pannier case—a sort of saddlebag for a mule—and they would pull him up on a separate rope while I followed, soothing the poor little fellow.

When I got to the bottom, though, Hank nearly tore my pant leg off. It became clear he was out of sorts and in no mood for a rescue, but what was I to do? Go back up and tell them to forget it? Tie the rope around his neck, maybe? Shoot him? None of those would exactly enhance the reputation of the Lander County Search and Rescue team, but this saddlebag thing wasn't going to work. Then Hank lunged and sunk his teeth into my calf. *Ouch!* I instinctively grabbed my hard hat and swung as hard as I could, bonking him squarely on the noggin. He let go and wobbled a bit as cartoon birdies fluttered around his head, and I wrapped and strapped him into that pannier case so fast I'd have won a buckle if we'd been at a rodeo. A vet examined him at the top and found that, other than a large lump on his head—apparently from falling down the mine shaft—Hank seemed to have come through the ordeal just fine.

Over the span of perhaps five years, the Lander County Search and Rescue unit participated in only one other incident that I remember, and I don't recall that the team was ever formally disbanded; it just sort of faded away gradually, in the same manner that my membership did.

Medical treatment also existed on a more social level. Although many rural areas now have at least a clinic, thanks to Nevada Health Centers, in years past the only medical treatment available was provided by volunteer ambulance services. Austin was no different, and until the mid-1970s we relied on individuals to take on the job voluntarily, going through whatever training they could find on their own, in order that the community might have a least some level of emergency medical care. These individuals were on a higher plane than I, for certain, and I suspect they were on a higher plane than most everybody else, too.

Later, the formal Emergency Medical Service, or EMS, was organized on a statewide level and began standardizing health care and training for volunteer ambulance services. A result of this was the first generation of certified emergency medical technicians. The concept came from, of all things, war. It was found that soldiers were surviving combat injuries that, away from the battlefield, were killing civilians. Not surprisingly, the reason was that combat medics and corpsmen were giving emergency treatment as soon as the injury occurred, while at home, especially in rural areas, capable medical treatment was often hours away. While there wasn't much that could be done to cut response time to accidents on lonely highways, the idea was that more-thorough care could be given to victims upon the arrival of the ambulance, rather than waiting until the patient was delivered to the hospital. The theory was that the sooner a victim was medically stabilized, even if it took longer at the accident site, the better off he'd be.

From that point on, all volunteer ambulance attendants of licensed services had to attend and complete basic EMT training. The early courses consisted of forty hours of classroom training, with a final requirement that each trainee spend one shift assisting in the emergency room of a city hospital during peak hours, such as a Friday or Saturday night.

The first EMT training in Austin was offered in the winter of 1981. I backed into it reluctantly, and only because I'd recently become a deputy sheriff. Having been raised mostly as a Christian Scientist, a religion that forbade doctors and medicine, the only first-aid schooling I'd ever had was a few hours in USMC recruit training, a period of my life that was blurry at best. When I found myself in the official position of being the first to the scene where people were busted up, I knew I had to get some skills that would allow me to do more than direct traffic, especially when where wasn't any traffic, and especially when the victims had to have help right now, this very moment. So I signed up for the EMT training, not as a principal, you understand, but more in the manner of a refugee hanging onto the end of the boat.

I tried not to show my astonishment when I first saw a diagram of a heart, because it didn't look anything like the box of Valentine candy that was referred to as heart-shaped. That kind of stuff kept me attentive to a fault, but I also had a tendency to get queasy and lightheaded during graphic exercises, and to counter these symptoms I was taught to drop my pencil. People faint because the blood drains out of their head, and if you bend over to where your head's low enough for gravity to bring it back, such as reaching down for your pencil, you recover.

Good training, by golly.

Surprisingly, I wasn't all that far behind most of my classmates, of whom there were about forty at the start, with my future wife, Val, among them. Only a dozen would make it all the way through, and I wasn't at all confident that I would be one of them. Val was more assured, although she didn't have much choice; her mother was one of the instructors. I stuck to her like glue.

Students came from all walks of life; firemen, ranchers, miners, housewives, clerks, teachers, businessmen, laborers, and of course cops. Most lived in Austin, but some were from Eureka and Round Mountain and the outlying ranches. The instructors came from as far as Elko, 150 miles distant, whether it was snowing or not, and the whole kit and caboodle, instructors and students alike, showed up at the Austin firehouse two nights a week every week for three months. "Duct Tape," a tall, lanky student whose real name I've long forgotten, stands out in my mind as a model sort of EMT graduate. He earned his nickname because of his extensive use of duct tape in class. One of the instructors had offhandedly mentioned that duct tape could be used, in a pinch, as regular first-aid tape to hold compresses on, etc. It was the "etc." that seemed to inspire Duct Tape, and he was never the same afterward. He carried a roll with him constantly, either in his medical bag or around his wrist like an oversized bracelet. Woe to the hapless victim in exercises to whom Duct Tape was assigned. Although the tape wasn't allowed on bare skin, everything else was open season, and many patients found themselves wearing more silver than the

Tin Man from Oz. When our exercises were timed, Duct Tape won easily, as nobody could Velcro as fast as he could tape. Because rolls of duct tape weren't carried in our inventory of medical supplies, he happily supplied his own, a case at a time no doubt.

When we got our assignments for the hospital I'm pretty sure the doctors took Duct Tape's duct tape away from him, but as a whole our group did well. Val even sewed up a cut lip, under a doctor's watchful gaze. Me, well, I was all thumbs and kept dropping my pencil, but the sun eventually rose on a new crop of EMTs. Nobody was more surprised than me to find I was one of them.

During the ten years that Val and I were EMTs with the Austin Ambulance, Terry Gandolfo (Val's mother) and Vicky Jones (Val's aunt) ran the service, making out schedules, ordering supplies, billing patients, dealing with the county commissioners, scheduling training, paying bills, maintaining the ambulances, and handling runs when the rest of us were unavailable. In short, they *were* the ambulance service, and we helped when we could.

Before paging units were available the only way to get a crew together was by telephone, with the dispatcher at the sheriff's office in Austin—or in Battle Mountain, after hours—working their way through the call list one by one until a driver and two EMT's were found. On occasion we had to shanghai a driver who wasn't actually authorized through EMS, but that seemed a better alternative than having only one attendant in back. I was shanghaied a couple of times myself before I became an EMT, so I knew how lonely it was behind the wheel when you didn't know what was going on, and we avoided it if at all possible. However, we once did wake a new off-duty deputy to drive when we were shorthanded, and much to his credit he jumped right in. Terry and I were in back, and we picked up two patients who had been involved in a car-cow collision 15 miles southeast of Austin on State Route 376. We transported them to the nearest hospital, which was in Tonopah, 120 miles south of Austin. By the time we finished up and headed home it was around three in the morning, and both Terry and I fell asleep on the gurneys in back. We awoke as the sun was coming up and were appalled to find we were just coming into Ely, which is 150 miles east of Austin. Deputy Wise had missed the turnoff to Austin coming out of Tonopah, simply because he'd never been there before. Still, we did get a good breakfast out of it at one of the casinos.

The locals rely on our ambulance as much, or more, than anybody. Although we now have a clinic, it's not surprising to find that illness and injury seldom strike during office hours. Therefore we still very much appreciate the folks who now give their time to the Austin Ambulance Service, and it's a real comfort to know we're still in good hands.

There are other organizations in town to which I've never belonged, and they have gotten along just fine without me, somehow. Easily the most visible is the Lions Club, and that's only partly because of the bright yellow vests the members wear. They also boast a matching plywood trailer, perhaps five feet wide by ten feet long, that always shows up at outdoor events in the summertime and is the place to go for cold refreshments on a hot day. Lions usually put on a barbecue or two at appropriate times, and members are regularly involved in organizing the Fourth of July street games. The Lions Club speech contest, which I've been honored to judge in the past, is an annual event for our high school students, the best of whom go on to district and then regional contests. The club is also generous when it comes to donating time and money to worthwhile causes, and often helps out as a group when the need arises.

Less visible, and much more secretive, is the local Masonic chapter. All I know about the Masons is that they've been around a long time and the members dress very nicely for meetings. The local Masonic Hall, located on Main Street between the Stagecoach Inn and the Austin Garage, is a beautiful old two-story brick building that, like Dick Clark, just doesn't seem to age. Also, with nothing more to back it up than my own observations, I believe the Order of the Eastern Star is a women's group—also well dressed—that is associated with the Masons. When they all meet in Austin, perhaps twice a year, it looks like an event you might expect to see in a less casual setting, like New York City, maybe.

There are several other, smaller organizations in Austin that appeal to a broad range of interests and whose meeting and event information is usually posted on the wall of the post office and at the courthouse: The Austin Roping Club hosts various horse-related events, such as barrel racing and team roping, at the Cass Alworth Rodeo Arena below town. There are bleachers for spectators, and a concession stand is manned for the larger events.

For firearms enthusiasts, the Pony Canyon Gun Club has a target and trapshooting range above the rodeo grounds, where turkey shoots are held. It sits near the site of the Nevada Central Railroad depot and, as revealed in old photographs, was once a popular spot for summer baseball contests. The early town of Clifton was situated along the canyon bottom from approximately the gun club trailer down to Big Creek Road.

The Austin Historical Society meets in the landmark Gridley Store to promote and preserve the history of the area and has been instrumental in placing several Austin buildings on the National Historic Register.

There is also the Sorority and the Red Hat Society, for women only—not that they'd have to post any Keep Out signs on my account—and kids can get involved with local chapters of the Boy Scouts, the Girl Scouts, or the 4-H.

There have been, during the decades I've lived here, forays by several less-formal clubs and groups that evaporated over time. In the '80s we had three or four pilots who flew out of the airport outside of town, and they banded together to form the Austin Air Force. Navy pilots train in central Nevada, and I often wondered what they thought when they looked down to see a tight formation of Cessnas and Ercoupes winging toward Fallon. Shivered in their boots, no doubt. I know we did.

About the time I arrived in Austin the citizens band radio craze was getting underway, and those of us who mounted the automobile versions beneath our dashboards came to form a loose sort of group, all identified by our respective "handles": "Breaker breaker one-nine this is Sandwalker . . . hey FiveCard, gotcher ears on?" My gosh, we must have driven the truckers, who used mobile CBs as part of their livelihood, absolutely nuts. If you stood back and took a sober view of it though, CB radios made good sense in the Great Basin Desert. They offered a limited version of what cell phones do today, and even an imperfect way of communicating across the vast, unpopulated reaches of central Nevada was preferable to being stuck in a wash somewhere with no way to summon help. I don't know why the CB fad died out around here as quickly as it did, which was very nearly overnight.

One of my favorites among the various ad hoc social groupings was the Sazerac Liars Club. It had been a popular organization in Austin a century earlier and was briefly reincarnated around 1975. Its purported leader, a temporary Austinite named Murph, stopped by the restaurant and actively recruited me while I was working on some breakdown or other. He had with him blank membership cards prominently stamped with the Sazerac Liars logo, letting all men know by these presents that the bearer was, by nature, unsavory.

"I don't know," I said to Murph, "I'm not much of a liar."

"Works for me," he said, filling out the card. "With that whopper, you're in. We'll be meeting here tonight at seven-thirty sharp."

Although I prepared a table for us, there was no meeting, as Murph was, of course, lying.

Austin does have annual social events that have to be planned and organized at particular times of the year, such as Gridley Days. Small committees—sometimes just a coordinator—exist for the few weeks that it takes to put together the specific event, and then they disband for the rest of the year. While the committee—or coordinator—initiates the event, the entire community usually ends up being involved in one way or another. Gridley Days, held on Father's Day weekend every June in memory of Red Cross benefactor Reuel Colt Gridley, is a prime example. A relatively recent town holiday (going back twenty-one years at this writing), the celebration has become the traditional kickoff to summer. Gridley Days has suffered greatly the past couple of years because it has coincided with the invasion of Mormon crickets, also a recent Austin event. Mormon crickets aren't Mormon, they're not even crickets, and maybe that contributes to their orneriness, but they are big and armored and ugly and downright unappetizing. It remains to be seen how Gridley Days will go if the insects aren't eliminated, which is doubtful because environmentalists are blocking the use of poisons that can eradicate them; the Mormon crickets, I mean, not the environmentalists. Unfortunately.

One event that won't ever be bothered by Mormon crickets is the town

Nativity, held a couple of weeks before Christmas. It has to be the most frigid live show ever produced, often taking place in single-digit weather, just as darkness falls. It is staged in the clinic parking lot across from the courthouse on Main Street, close to the center of town, and the set is erected the day before showtime so that the parking lot isn't tied up any longer than necessary. The story is unquestionably the thing, beginning with Joseph and Mary's arrival in Bethlehem and ending with the three wise men bringing their gifts to baby Jesus, but there's no denying that the props and the animals, which include live camels and donkeys, get a lot of crowd attention.

The background music and actor dialogue are prerecorded so that they don't get drowned out by passing hay trucks, but the hymns are sung by locals, as is the chorus, supplemented in recent years by the Battle Mountain High School choir. Hay bales, stacked in a wall some fifteen feet high and topped with an electric "star in the east," frame the manger, and the costumes and the music and the camels and the lighting are nothing short of majestic. It is certain to give you goose bumps if the weather hasn't already.

Afterward the firehouse is opened for hot chocolate and homemade cookies while names are drawn for winners in the annual turkey raffle, followed by the announcement of the best decorations of the Christmas home-and-business lighting contest. All in all, Austin's Nativity offers one of the most moving nights of the season, anywhere, and even though the presentation varies little from year to year, you never grow tired of it. Val, my wife, has been the coordinator of the show for the past several years, and every one of those years she's tried to talk me into impersonating a wise man in order to get me to ride one of the camels down Fourth Street to the manger. She's had no luck so far, which makes me a lot wiser than most.

Because Austin is such a tight-knit community, when tragedy strikes one of us it ripples out to all. Funerals are generally held at one of the churches or the town hall, whichever is appropriate, and occasionally at the high school gymnasium. Most everybody in town makes it a point to attend if at all possible, and many who have moved away come back for the services of old friends. Afterward refreshments are often served at the town hall, which allows family and friends to spend more time together than would otherwise be possible. There's an air of genuine sadness about the whole thing, but at the same time there is something wonderful about the closeness we all share.

Shortly after Val's thirty-fifth birthday she was diagnosed with a brain tumor, a serious one that required the operation be performed at a top facility—in her case, Presbyterian University Hospital in Pittsburgh, Pennsylvania. We were stunned and almost immobile from the shock of it all, and here came Austin to the rescue. These folks started right in making preparations to help with the family while Val and I were gone, which turned out to be almost an entire month, and Val's cousin, Lane Maestretti, came up with two round-trip airline tickets. Friends and family and acquaintances put on fundraisers and provided enough money for my stay at a motel and for meals. All we had to do was go. Upon our return the various churches and organizations had a schedule worked out to take turns bringing cooked dinners to the house every evening throughout the winter. If I hadn't gone through it myself, I don't know if I would have believed that so much generosity and compassion could be generated in an area of eight hundred people, and it eventually extended throughout Lander County. Val came through it all right, although she lost some of her sight and hearing on the right side. I thought it would be impossible, but she went back to teaching long before the school year was out, due in no small part to the outpouring of help and prayers we received from the community. That was more than fifteen years ago, and I'm still amazed at the extent of these people's support for us. But that is what they do, it is what they are. I thank God every day for them, and for the town in which they live.

PEOPLE

A town is a location for sure, but more than that, it's a collection of people. I loved the looks of Austin the moment I set eyes on it, the pleasant canyon setting and the old buildings, but if the locals had been grumpy and surly I certainly wouldn't have moved here. It is said that happiness is a state of mind, not a place and not people, and I believe that. Still, it's been my experience that your surroundings and the people therein do eventually seep into your attitude, which is why you seldom see commuters enjoying a routine traffic jam on the way to work.

The people who live in Austin and whom I was fortunate enough to run into and come to know are the subjects of this chapter. They are not necessarily the movers and the shakers, or the officials, or the business owners, or the natives, or even popular. They are the folks who made an indelible imprint on my life here, the ones you're likely to meet if you move to a small community in the middle of the desert.

Carol Mendenhall owned Carol's Country Store on Main Street, a refurbished dry goods store on the way to its next calling, and she greeted us like long-lost cousins the first time we stopped. A bleached blonde, Carol was a recent transplant from the big city and was so passionate about Austin that you couldn't help but get caught up in her enthusiasm. It was the first time I encountered a phenomenon that I later found typical among new residents, including me: There is a time after you move here during which happiness is indeed a place, and the place has a name, and the name is Austin, and as long as you are in Austin you will be happy. This is a bubble that has no choice but to burst, and it's amazing that nobody ever sees it coming. The bubble lasts for two years, almost exactly, and when it does burst you can't get out of here fast enough. Those who truly fit will leave for however long it takes us to remember what it's like outside the remains of the bubble, maybe a season, and then we'll come back for good, this time without cartoon music in the background. Carol's own particular bubble was still several months from bursting when Marlys and I entered the picture, so the three of us cavorted happily amid our schemes and dreams and plans.

Carol introduced us to the gentleman who owned the building we ended up buying. It was Carol who suggested we turn the ground floor into some kind of a business, and it was Carol who helped us move in, and it was Carol who introduced us to the locals, and it was Carol who really broke the ice for our lives here. She married Bill Givens, a local who also became a good friend and who in turn introduced me to the immediate countryside. Bill was an old area rancher who owned Carol's building and moved into town when ranching was no longer practical for him. Newcomers to any place almost have to have a Carol and Bill if they're going to get settled in quickly; they're like sponsors.

John Nagy was a fellow about my age we met while playing blackjack one night at Clara's Golden Club, and whom we sort of adopted into the family. John lived in the building next to the Golden Club with his father, Gabe, and his brother, Sonny. They worked at odd jobs around town whenever they weren't prospecting the hills for whatever riches they might stumble upon, just like hundreds of Austinites before them. I think they were originally from Montana, where Gabe had worked as a miner, but I never found out how they came to be in Austin. I had discovered by the time I met them that if the locals wanted you to know their story, they'd volunteer it.

When John discovered we were turning the Stagecoach Inn into an ice cream parlor he nodded his approval and, without being asked, just showed up the following morning and helped me map out a plan to attack the walls. He became a regular helper after that and was the main reason we were able to open for business as quickly as we did. The funny thing was, I never did ask for his help; he just kept showing up and pitching in. We became good friends and often tipped a few brews—OK, maybe several—as we worked late into the night. When we built the restrooms, we filled the walls with empty beer cans—for insulation, you see—and even threw in a treasure map for good measure. We figured that might be a real hoot far into the next century when somebody tore out that wall. Har har. It didn't quite happen like that; some thirty years later the new owner, Jan Morrison, came up to the judge's chamber where I was the judge and told me she'd gotten a real kick out of that map. And the beer cans. Oops.

When we reached the point where we could take a day off now and then, John took us to some interesting places around Austin. One was on a hilltop just northeast of town, where he showed us some strange petroglyphs. Petroglyphs are carvings on rocks, and in this part of the world they were typically made ages ago by Indians (one famous site is thirty miles east of Austin at Hickison Summit). But the petroglyphs John showed us were different. They looked to be fairly recent because of their design. There were several pictures, all of them more cartoon than primitive. One portrayed the profile of a man's head blowing what appear to be bubbles, while another depicted a leg obviously broken in at least a compound fracture with the foot, complete with four little toes, twisted backward. Ouch. No wonder he was blowing bubbles.

John also showed us a rock arrastra he'd found overgrown with brush in a canyon bottom. Used to crush ore and regularly employed by early Spaniards, an arrastra consisted of a flat rock floor perhaps five or six feet across, with a hole in the center that held a wooden post. The outer edge was walled by a circle of rocks about a foot high, leaving a round bowl where the ore was placed. A crossbeam attached to the central post overhung the rock wall in such a manner that a mule could be harnessed to it. A large rock was hung from the crossbeam inside the wall and dragged in a circle by the mule until the ore was crushed to a more or less powdery fineness. When water was added to this grit to make a slurry, the heavier particles—those bearing the gold or silver—tended to sink to the lowest parts of the arrastra, including into the cracks in the stone floor. Although American prospectors borrowed the idea in the 1800s, John thought that this particular arrastra was indeed built by early Spaniards, and he showed us what appeared to be the head of a broad Spanish battle-ax he'd found in the area. I didn't know what to think of it then, and I don't know what to think of it now, but John had more great tales to tell than anybody I'd ever known. As with most of my early Austin friends, we drifted apart after I became a deputy sheriff, and I've always regretted that.

Joe Dory owned Dory's Chevron station on the west edge of town, and his sister, Jennifer, ran the adjoining Pony Canyon Motel. They'd been tragically orphaned while in high school when an airplane crash near Jarbidge, Nevada, claimed the lives of their parents, Joe and Elaine Dory. Joe and Jennifer inherited the businesses at that point and ran them for years afterward. Joe is one of those people who can play the guitar and the banjo and the fiddle and the piano—in short, just about anything musical that drifts by. I can play the guitar, and I can play the jukebox. That's it. That was enough, though, to get us playing music together. It was a common practice at the time for anyone who could play an instrument to jam down at the Golden Club whenever the spirits moved, so to speak, which was quite often. I enjoyed it hugely, but I think after a couple hours we reached a point of spirit saturation where we became somewhat unmusical. Didn't bother us, but Clara no doubt lost some business now and then.

Joe was also given to adventure, and he spent his spare time flying airplanes or riding motorcycles, always keeping an eye out for anything else that might spice up the day. One of these anything elses was hang gliding. When hang gliders first came out, Joe and two other locals, Jerry Mock and Jay Winrod, pooled their money and bought one. Before many flights went by, Jay was wearing pins in his wrist and his third of the hang glider was up for sale. I wasn't interested, but I ended up going hang gliding with Joe at Sand Mountain anyway, because his enthusiasm was so darn infectious. As its name implies, Sand Mountain is a huge sand dune. Some seventy-five miles west of Austin just north of Highway 50, it towers several hundred feet above the valley floor and is paradise to dune buggy enthusiasts and others for whom life is but a dream. Needless to say I hurt myself, though not fatally, and not to the extent that I needed pins to hold my joints together. I felt bad about bending the glider, but not bad enough to invest in it; after all, I was bent every bit as much as it was. After that I steered clear of Joe's enthusiasm. It was apparent that I was blessed with as little sense as he was, given the right conditions.

Another Joe had a major impact on my first years in Austin: Joe Ramos. I first met Ramos when he was delivering propane around town. Shortly thereafter he introduced me to shotgunning in general, and chukar hunting in particular.

More than anybody I've ever known, Ramos enjoyed staying busy; whether at work or play didn't seem to make any difference. That mindset was, and still is, foreign to me, so it apparently doesn't rub off, thank goodness. When I gave up my job managing the Chevron bulk plant below town, Ramos took it over, and since he already knew where all the ranches were, it was a pretty seamless transfer. I stayed on as relief driver and filled in at the plant whenever he needed me, if I wasn't off on another part-time job. When his station wasn't busy and he saw we were up to something at the Stagecoach Inn, Joe often walked across the street and helped out at whatever we happened to be doing. One of these occasions entailed laying a cement floor for a walk-in refrigerator behind the restaurant. When Joe saw the cement truck pull up and stop on the road above and behind our place, he showed up in time to find me standing inside the forms, watching in disbelief as the liquefied concrete climbed above my ankles. I was overwhelmed with cement, literally. I never would have believed it could come out of the truck that fast. When I looked up, Joe tossed me a shovel and said, "This isn't one of those jobs you can take all day about, Andersen."

Then he jumped in with me and we got the cement spread out before it started hardening. Ramos didn't save my life—I'm sure I would have climbed out of there on my own—but he undoubtedly saved the floor, no small consequence.

In the fire department Ramos and I, along with Paul Saralegui, a lanky kid who was more at home on a horse than on a fire truck, formed a loose sort of Three Amigos. As chief, secretary, and assistant chief, respectively, we ended up doing a lot of the administrative work together and became good friends. We attended everything from training sessions to turkey shoots, often traveling as far as Carson City. And if chukar partridge have memories, I'm sure they learned to avoid us in the field, not for our hunting prowess, but because we just had too much fun.

Andy and Gloria Kaltenbach owned the Frontier Tavern, twelve miles east of Austin at the junction of Highway 50 and State Route 8A South (which was later designated State Route 376). The Frontier was much more than a tavern; it was a restaurant, motel, gas station, truck stop, garage, and tow service. The first time I stopped in, Andy's tow truck was down with a busted winch drum, and I was a welder by trade. How could we *not* get along?

Andy and Gloria split the business duties in the way that Marlys and I would later adopt; she took care of the food and cleaning while he kept the equipment and facilities maintained and running. Both were full-time jobs in any business, but with all the Frontier had going they put in a full day for sure, even with hired help. Andy got his fuel by tanker truck from Sacramento, but occasionally he'd run dry and have us deliver from the bulk plant in Austin. Because there were times when a driver wasn't available right away, Andy had a key so he could load and deliver his own fuel in emergencies. It worked out just fine, and Andy in fact made a couple of deliveries for me out in his direction when things got tight, which would probably raise eyebrows anywhere else. In return, I took care of any welding he needed help with.

Andy had been an officer with the Colorado Highway Patrol, and because of his experience seldom had to call for a deputy when trouble broke out at his bar. When I later joined the sheriff's department, his expertise came in handy several times. During the Henson murder investigation, when we had a truckload of evidence towed to the Reno crime lab, Andy was driving the tow truck. I followed him in a patrol vehicle, and when we were finished we met at a pizza parlor for dinner. Andy excused himself from the table for what seemed like a lengthy time, but I'd been working so many long days and was so tired that I didn't pay much attention. When we left and walked out to the parking lot, my patrol car was hanging off the end of Andy's tow truck like a trophy bluefin tuna. He motioned for me to climb into the cab with him, tossed me a can of beer, and told me he'd wake me when we got to Austin. Good man, Andy. He and Gloria sold the Frontier and moved away around 1984. The place stood vacant for a while and then burned to the ground one night. It was never rebuilt, and today a private home occupies the site, which I still think is the best business location in the state of Nevada. The last time I saw Andy was when he came up to Austin for a visit in the late '90s. He gave me his address in Reno, but in the manner of all who are burdened with things that need to be done, I was always just a little too busy to look him up.

Harry and Linda McCoy weren't locals, but they'd been in Austin a few days and happened to stop by the Stagecoach Inn the morning John and I were redesigning the ground floor. Harry was balding and heavyset and looked like he should be driving a cab in Hawthorne, which was, of course, what he'd last done. Linda was blonde and a bit shorter than Harry and looked like a waitress who might run off with a cab driver, which, of course, she was. Linda and Marlys hit it off immediately, and Marlys took her on a tour of the building while Harry just walked right over and joined in our planning session. I'm not too modest to admit that I was pleased when Harry doubled the crew I would later be in charge of, because with their muscle and my supervising skills the walls wouldn't have a chance. As soon as we had a general idea of the destruction we wanted to work, we took a break, and out of generosity I invited them over to the ice chest early; that is, before lunch.

The following week Harry and Linda took us up on an offer of a second-floor room in exchange for their help. They ended up staying with us for three years, lending a hand or several hands daily and even running the place when Marlys and I took time off. I don't know what we would have done without them, and I never understood how it came to be that they just walked in like that, out of nowhere—or Hawthorne, if you prefer—right when we needed them. John had done the exact same thing, and it was getting too crowded to call it coincidence. There was no way, financially, we could have hired the help we needed and they supplied, and that's when I first felt a little tugging of something at work far beyond my comprehension. I wasn't ready, at the time, to call it God.

Lee and Rene Maestretti ran the Austin Light and Power Company, which provided all of Austin's electrical needs before Sierra Pacific brought in store-bought power in 1975. They lived directly across Main Street from the Stagecoach Inn and were very supportive of our attempts to establish a new business in town. Lee carried a full line of electrical supplies in the Austin Garage, where the massive generators were housed, and was always helpful in finding what I needed to take care of the electrical problems that have a way of materializing in old buildings. Our building turned out to have the bare minimum electrical service, naturally, so we were going to have to upgrade to a commercial entry box with its associated expensive innards before we could even think of putting in restaurant equipment. Lee, wearing his trademark khaki work clothes and baseball cap, leather tool pouch hanging from his belt, came over and figured out what we'd need. His list grew longer and longer as he walked around in back, and he when finally handed me his estimate, I squinted my eyes in hopes of making it hurt less. But it came to $80, total. On top of that, he and his son, Stan, brought all the stuff over—brand-new, still in boxes—and showed me how it all went together. For $80. Where I came from, you couldn't even buy the permit for that.

Lee and Rene often came over for dinner after we opened. They were obviously unused to seeing overhead lights controlled by a dimmer switch, because the first night they were in the restaurant I dimmed the lights as I always did and Lee jumped from his booth and ran out the front door. I asked Rene what was up, and she, looking concernedly at the lights, said, "Something's wrong with the generator." It doesn't get much better than that, and after the dust settled we laughed until our sides hurt, Lee included. He never quite got used to the lights dimming like that, and even though he never ran out the door again, he always gave an involuntary little start whenever the lights went down. I couldn't help but watch, and he always looked over and gave me a little wave and a sheepish grin.

I couldn't have done that, any of it, with the Sierra Pacific Power Company.

Kittie Bonner was old when I got here, but she sure didn't act like it. She had a rambling old house on the northwest corner of Main and Pine streets, where she gave haircuts from a genuine leather barber's chair in her living room. Kittie had achieved a measure of fame when, upon her husband's death, she took over his duties as constable in Austin, thereby becoming the first female law officer in Nevada, at least, and possibly the nation. She painted in both oils and watercolors, mostly horses, which she loved. One of her paintings was of a filly I boarded for the short time Marlys and I spent as a caretakers of a cabin at Lynch Creek. The horse belonged to Cindy Jolly, a local who'd allowed me to ride it in a Pony Express rerun. The painting still hangs today on the wall of the International Cafe and is captioned "Flecka," which of course was the horse's name, although I always thought it was "Flicka," as in the book *My Friend Flicka*.

Kittie's paintings, and her poems, and the tales she told of dry camps and chasing mustangs, reflected her great love of Nevada and the Great Basin desert country. You couldn't help but get caught up in it yourself, and she left me with a greater appreciation of the desert than I'd had before, which is saying something.

We met Betty McKnight while she was bartending at the Austin Hotel. She called everybody "Curly"—especially bald Harry—and if she discerned even the slightest bit of guff about you, she'd bring out her flyswatter and slap you silly. After stints at the Austin and the International she ran Betty's Bar, which is now the Owl Club, but she eventually came to work for us as a cook, and a darn good one, at the Stagecoach Inn. The tables slowly turned over the years, and Betty herself gradually became known as Curly, a title she still carries today. She has a different flyswatter, but it feels exactly the same as the first one, I can tell you from experience. Curly came to Austin from Beatty, and she was eventually joined here by her son Rick and daughters Roxanna, who serves as Austin's postmaster today, and Theresa. Theresa gave me fits when I was a deputy, once unsnapping a dump pouch on my duty belt while I was making a bar check at the Golden Club. Six .38-caliber bullets dropped onto the floor, and I'm here to tell you there is no graceful way for a deputy to retrieve his bullets from a barroom floor. You just have to Barney-Fife your way through. It was a good lesson, though, and it changed the way I carried extra bullets; I always thought Theresa would have made a good lecturer at the police academy.

Rick Banovich was transferred to Austin as the resident trooper for the Nevada Highway Patrol shortly after I arrived. Rumor had it that he'd once given his wife, Brenda, a speeding ticket. Once I got to know Rick, I didn't doubt it; he was tough but fair, and since everybody was treated the same there really wasn't much to complain about if he ticketed you. He was a friend of Joe Ramos, and on occasion we'd all hang out at Ramos's station on summer evenings, enjoying the weather and tipping a few. President Carter's brother, Billy, had a reputation for doing the same thing at his gas station in Georgia, and except for the peanuts I imagine it would have been difficult to tell us apart, from a distance.

I'd never been as relaxed or as comfortable as I was on those evenings, and I believe if nothing else in Austin had worked out for me, those simple gatherings would have made the whole move worthwhile. As it turned out, of course, most things did work out, and when I went to work as a deputy a couple of years later, Rick took me under his wing. I rode with him as much as I could, and after watching him on traffic stops I patterned my approach on his. No matter how grumpy the driver was initially—and some of them were *really* grumpy—when Rick was finished and handed him his citation, it always ended with a "Thank you, officer," followed by the driver smiling and waving as he pulled away. You'd have thought he'd won the raffle.

I was told Doc Allen wasn't really a doctor, but I never found out how he got the name. He was an older fellow, kind of frail looking, and was always pleasant and quiet when he came into the restaurant. He once asked if I would help him patch a leak in his roof, as he was too old to climb around up there anymore. I agreed to do it, but when I got to his house, which was far older than he was, and saw how steeply the roof was pitched, I started waffling. Doc shrugged and said it wasn't a problem; he had a "roof ladder."

Roof ladder? He brought out a regular wooden ladder, perhaps fourteen feet long, that had two short pieces of two-by-fours bolted at right angles to the ends of the uprights, forming little hooks that would reach over the peak of the roof and hold the ladder in place. I could see it would make a safe and sane perch from which to make repairs, so I stopped looking for an escape clause. We leaned an extension ladder against the eaves, and I climbed up so I could haul the roof ladder up and over the peak, hook-ing it securely in place. It seemed solid, so with a pail of patch cement in one hand I started up the steeply pitched tin roof. I didn't notice that the roof itself was sagging badly, and even if I had noticed, I doubt if I would have realized that my weight would bend the ladder inward so far that the hooks would be lifted away from the peak, freeing the ladder and turning it into a sled.

There wasn't time to think, but I do remember the ladder and I plunging over the edge, and I remember bracing myself for the crash, and then not crashing. Doc Allen, frail old guy that he was, caught that ladder and me—with the pail of roof-patch cement still clutched in my hand—in mid-air and lowered us gently to the ground.

"Nice catch," I said, unable to think of anything more appropriate. To this day I don't know where Doc found the strength, or the reflexes, to do that, and he was never able to explain it either. We didn't get his roof fixed that day, but it did appear that good intentions would be rewarded in Austin.

Hugo Ostberg was also getting up there in years, but he was still doing rockwork when we were looking to refurbish the front of the restaurant. His work was on display at the Forest Service building, as well as several other places around town. Hugo used wonderstone, a flat, colorful type of shalelike rock, to face over any flat surface, including walls, for a durable and nice-looking exterior. He was a heavyset fellow who always wore a pushed-back baseball cap above a perpetual smile, and he spoke with a heavy Scandinavian accent—so heavy that at times I had no idea what he was talking about. For instance, when I showed him the wall around the front door, including the overhead, and asked if he could make the rock stay up there, he said yes, that he used sheeken var and had never had a problem with the rock falling.

Sheeken var? I'd never heard of it.

"Hyou know," he said, "sheeken var!" Then he tucked his hands beneath his arms, started flapping his elbows, and strutted around snapping his head forward in a pecking motion. Even tourists slowed to watch.

Oh! Chicken wire! Since he was already good for business, I hired him on the spot.

Hugo drove a brown stepside pickup that apparently wouldn't go over two miles per hour, and I never once saw him look over his shoulder before pulling out of a parking spot. To my knowledge he never had a wreck and he never caused one, but there were times, when summer tourist traffic was heavy, that he looked like he was leading a crawling parade of campers and motor homes through town. Because a lot of them gave up and parked, Hugo was indeed good for business.

Connie Stewart was a promoter, which every mining town past, present, or future had, has, or will have. What he promoted was the bottom of the canyon below town, and he made a pretty good living at it. Shoot, *I* made a pretty fair living from it for a couple of months. A century's worth of tailings, carrying a minute cargo of silver from the mines above, had washed into the floor of Pony Canyon and, eventually, into Connie's future sphere of promotion. The problem was in separating the silver from the dirt in a profitable manner. Connie came up with several schemes and managed to find eager financing for every one of them, but the funny thing is that Connie wasn't running a scam; he was the biggest believer of them all. He was always one idea away from rich. When I came in, which would correspond to the middle of the movie, Connie had engineered a plan to recover the silver by some metallurgical procedure that required three very huge V-shaped troughs fashioned out of 12-gauge sheet metal. He wanted me to do the welding for him and said the troughs would have to hold water without any leaks. I told him they wouldn't have to hold for very long, because the troughs wouldn't be stout enough to support the weight of the water. He needed heftier steel. But Connie roughed out a sketch of stiffeners and braces and tie rods that he claimed would provide added support, and his calculations showed that if dirt was backfilled around the troughs as they filled with water, they would hold. Besides that, he added, "I already bought the metal."

It wasn't so much what he said as the way he said it, and I would come to understand that this, not engineering, was Connie's gift. He could talk a snake out of its rattles and they'd both come away convinced things would get better from that point on.

It took three of us working full-time several weeks to build the troughs, and when we were done, Connie threw us a party. But when they were filled with water, in spite of his precautions he ended up with three muddy holes full of buckled and twisted sheet metal punctuated with an occasional iron rod poking skyward. It was the final straw for Connie. He left soon after that, and so did my co-workers, and so, I assume, did the investors. Not me, though. I sat on the hillside above the abandoned site and modified the last line of the old song "Big John": "At the bottom of this pit lies a big, big, scam."

I wasn't leaving, no sir; I wasn't about to miss any of this stuff.

Cass Alworth, for whom Austin's rodeo arena is named, was a well-liked buckaroo who lived out his final days in town. He had one glass eye, and with his matching one-tune harmonica stuck forever on "Red River Valley," he personified the Old West as I always imagined it. Cass once told me about a couple of wizened old cowboys he'd known who were taking turns running cattle through a chute, using a newfangled electric cattle prod to keep them moving. One of the steers, clearly not enjoying himself, reared up and fell over backward, landing on the cowboy in the chute and busting him up pretty good. A bystander got the ambulance from town, and as the injured cowboy was hauled away the remaining buckaroo commented, "Coulda been worse."

The bystander, agreeing, said, "Yeah, he could have been killed."

The cowboy studied the cattle in the chute for a moment and mused, "Worser than that; coulda been me."

That second cowboy seemed a likely counterpart for Cass, as that's the way he looked at things. He certainly never fretted away any hours worrying about being politically correct. There were just too many things to be done, and he wanted to get in on as many as he could.

Me too.

Finally, a year after Marlys and I split up, I met Valerie Gandolfo. I knew her mother, Terry, who ran the ambulance service along with Vicky Jones, and I knew her father, Ron, the Austin postmaster. Val had moved back to Austin while I was on an extended vacation. She had taken part-time work as the relief dispatcher at the sheriff's office, but that wasn't where I met her, even though by then I was a deputy again. The first time I saw her I was on the night shift and making a routine bar check at the International. I asked to see her ID because she didn't look old enough to be in there. She was.

A few days later she was working in the office, filling in for Billie. Some major incident had brought all the bigwigs down from Battle Mountain, and the sheriff and undersheriff, along with two or three other deputies and myself, were discussing some serious law enforcement issues while Val took notes on the typewriter. The way everybody was positioned, I was the only one who could see her, and when I glanced at her she was grinning back at me with a gummed label stuck to the end of her nose.

It would take a few years, but after that how could I *not* marry her?

TIME OFF

I'd always wanted to blur the line between work and play so there wouldn't be that awful dread of punching the clock. Austin came as close as was possible, I think, because I'd often find work just sort of trailing into party time, first as we were turning our building into a restaurant, and later as I got used to jobs being under my control instead of vice versa. You have to make a living no matter what, of course, but if you're like me, the mere thought that you *have* to be at a particular place at a particular time doing a particular thing makes you queasy and quite often surly. Therefore, "getting out of California" had a meaning, for me, beyond leaving the state. It meant figuring out a way to enjoy most of my life, rather than little spurts here and there. In that sense I really branched out when I got here, but it wasn't easy, and at times I needed a little help.

After our initial burst of workworkwork energy, both Marlys and I finally noticed that we could, if we wanted, take time off whenever we wished. Although the reality of having to make a living kept our minds wonderfully focused, we did start taking off evenings just to have fun; on occasion we played blackjack at the Golden Club, we played pool at Vance and Arlene's Saloon, we played shuffleboard at Betty's Bar, and we played slot machines at the International. Not a lot, but enough so that we knew we were in charge. It was heady stuff to us recovering clock-punchers.

Bill Givens had introduced us to fishing at Big Creek, twelve miles south of Austin, and if we took a whole day off that's where we went, every time. It was delicious, being able to angle for trout less than a half hour from the front door. We did that, weather permitting, for close to a year.

Sometime afterward, my brother-in-law from Oregon was riding with me in the fuel truck as we inched our way up Austin Summit one summer day. He was gazing at the scenery on the passenger side, including a dirt road angling up the far side of Pony Canyon, and he casually asked, "Where does that road go?" I glanced over at it, having driven past it perhaps a hundred times. Shoot, since I'd moved to Austin I'd worked several odd jobs, of which delivering fuel to ranches was only the most recent, and because I was also transforming an old building into a restaurant I didn't have much enthusiasm for driving down dirt roads.

"I don't know," I replied, just as casually. Jim sat there awhile, still staring out the window, and then he added, "I believe if I lived here, I'd know where that road went."

I think it's called an epiphany, the sudden wave of realization that sweeps over you unbidden, out of nowhere. I looked again at the road he was referring to and noticed that it cut through the lower sections of two stands of trees before cresting through some rock outcroppings and disappearing over the top. Why in heck *didn't* I know where it went? I'd quit a good job in sunny California to move to the middle of Nevada, surrounding myself with thousands of square miles of uncluttered beauty, and for the most part I'd been ignoring it.

Unlike paved roads, which generally connect two known locations in the straightest line possible given man's construction abilities, dirt roads meander around all over the place. They have to because, like game trails, they follow the easiest natural corridor to wherever they're going, which may not be evident even after you get there; although most dirt roads have a purpose, some do not and just end with no explanation and no apology, leaving you alone on the top of a hill or at the end of a canyon. That's OK, that's why Detroit made four-wheel-drive vehicles, after all, and the end of a dirt road is often the beginning of a great day.

When Jim and Jean returned to visit the following year, we all piled into my truck and I drove up the very road that Jim had pointed out to start this whole thing. We came out at Birch Creek on the other side of the Toiyabe Mountains, a beautiful place. I turned to Jim and said, "There. Now you know."

"Know what?" he asked, clearly puzzled.

"Know where the road goes," I explained.

"What road?"

"This road," I said, exasperated. "You wanted to know where it went."

"No I didn't."

"Then why did you ask?"

"Ask what?"

"Ask . . . never mind." It was obvious that Jim didn't remember anything about it, and that's the way it is with epiphanies. They're very personal, and if you try to explain them, nobody but you will ever know what you're talking about. That's how I got like this, and that's why I drive down every dirt road I come across now.

Off-road four-wheeling, a by-product of dirt roads, was fun and invaluable too, because tucked over the next hill we found areas of downed and dead trees that furnished us with firewood for years to come, and we found stands of piñon pine that were fairly bursting with pine nuts, and we found rock ruins that were great fun to explore. In short, we found Nevada. It's away from the asphalt.

Getting firewood was, for me, relaxing. Whether I did it with family, with friends, or alone, I always enjoyed it. It typically took eight pickup loads of dead firewood to get through a winter because our fireplace, though cheerful, wasn't very efficient. My pickup held about half a cord, which by my count took an average of ten piñon trees to obtain. Piñons are small, but even so, that's about eighty downed trees a year I hauled out of the forest, which is one heck of a lot of clutter.

Initially I mounted my firewood expeditions under the flag of a free-use permit from the U.S. Forest Service. It seemed to me at the time that getting a free-use permit would eventually lead to paying for a permit, but the district ranger assured me that the Forest Service had no such intentions. The permits, he insisted, were purely for the purpose of gathering statistics. However, it came as no surprise when, a few years later, free-use permits fell by the wayside and woodcutters had to start paying for the privilege of cleaning dead fuel out of the forest.

I didn't stop laying in firewood until I noticed it was no longer fun, in my twentieth year of woodcutting. Summer lightning still starts fires in the mountains around here, but thanks to my efforts there are about sixteen hundred fewer dead trees to feed those fires. Smokey the Bear, indeed.

Occasionally—not very often, but occasionally—in isolated regions like this, a remote ranch or cabin becomes available for caretaking, an arrangement whereby somebody is allowed to live in a place in exchange for keeping it maintained and inhabited. A small cabin at Lynch Creek, owned by an out-of-state resident named Teleford Work, was beginning to fall into disrepair from neglect, and word got around that Mr. Work was looking for someone to live up there as a caretaker; fix the fences, maybe paint the place. Lynch Creek ran out of the Toiyabe Mountains about seventeen miles southeast of Austin in Smoky Valley. It was in a typical mountain canyon, meaning that over the millennia the creek's scouring action formed the canyon by dumping millions of tons of dirt and rock into the plain below, creating the alluvial fan that you see spilling out into the valley today. The cabin itself was located where the canyon opened into the top of the fan, perhaps two hundred feet above the valley floor, at the end of a two-mile dirt road that ascended from State Route 376, which ran the length of Smoky Valley, stringing the bases of the alluvial fans together like charms on a bracelet. The view from the cabin overlooking Smoky Valley was spectacular, from Highway 50 to the north all the way past Round Mountain some sixty miles south. Beyond the valley to the east rose the staggered peaks of the Toquima Mountain Range, forming an uneven fence along the horizon.

Although Marlys and I didn't realize it, we were nearing the point of disenchantment with Austin that all newcomers seem to reach after about two years, so the chance to get out of town came along at the perfect time. After talking with Mr. Work by telephone we landed the caretaking job at Lynch Creek. During the time we lived there, one or the other of us commuted to town almost every day to help with the restaurant, but Harry and Linda ran it well without need of supervision. Good thing, too, because the cabin had no telephone with which to contact us. It had no electricity either, but it did have running water piped in from the creek. It also had a cooking stove, a water heater, and a refrigerator, all powered by propane. Propane wasn't delivered; we used twenty-gallon portable tanks that we refilled in Austin. I'd never heard of a propane refrigerator—I mean, a refrigerator with a pilot light?— but it used ammonia as the refrigerant and turned out to be very efficient.

Water that wasn't used in the house, which was most of it, was piped on through to a manmade pond situated about twenty yards in front of, and below, the cabin. The pond covered roughly a quarter of an acre and was completely full in the early spring, when we moved in. Someone had built a small dock out of planks à la Huckleberry Finn, complete with a wooden raft tied alongside, and I frittered away more than a few summer days playing hooky out there. I never did like the ring of a telephone, so life without one was pure bliss for me, although Marlys missed it because of her kids back in California. As for electricity, I missed that only because the light from kerosene lamps was impossible to read by for very long. Other than that, I didn't feel at all inconvenienced.

Marlys tended a vegetable garden that did very well, and I rebuilt an old cedar-post structure and turned it into a chicken coop. We brought some Rhode Island Red chicks from Fallon so we could have fresh eggs, and between the chickens and the garden we began to attract some serious pests. I shot a lot of garden rodents that summer, but the chickens were assaulted in the middle of the night, and by the time I grabbed my rifle and flashlight and stumbled sleepily out there, the intruder was invariably gone. All I could do was try to reinforce the fencing so the thieves couldn't tunnel under it, and I was never entirely successful. All in all, though, it's surprising how much individuals can do to sustain themselves. With the help of a propane refrigerator.

The water heater was located next to the side door, which opened from the kitchen onto the garden. Somehow, a skunk got inside the house one day and hid behind the heater, for a while anyway. It was brought to my attention by Marlys's scream, which almost caused me to fall off the raft. By the time I got to shore and into the kitchen, the skunk was standing balanced on its forepaws like an acrobat, chattering and making some kind of a clicking noise. I picked up the broom and tried to shoo him out the doorway, but he took it personally, I guess, and fired on us. Then he skittered back behind the water heater. It was awful. I got my .22 rifle, as it was readily apparent that we were going to have to carry him out feet first, but my eyes were watering so badly that I was afraid to shoot toward the propane lines at the foot of the heater. I had to wait for him to come out onto the floor again, and before I finally got a shot, he'd fired a couple more bursts. The old homestead was very nearly inhabitable by the time I dispatched him. In desperation I burned several highway flares in the kitchen in hope of deodorizing the place, and it worked to the extent that the atmosphere was eventually more sulfur than skunk, but it took several weeks before the kitchen was anywhere near being mountain-air fresh again.

On another occasion I was stepping off the front porch when a very large snake came out from under the house, heading sluggishly toward the pond. When I noticed the head was flat and triangular in the manner of a rattlesnake, I ran for the gun cabinet again and grabbed the shotgun. I shot the snake before it could get into the brush, but the shot pattern at that range vaporized its head, unfortunately for my later curiosity as well as for the reptile. What was left was over five feet long, but it wasn't a rattlesnake. The tail came to a slender point, and the markings were not of a diamondback or anything else that I'd seen. Only pit vipers, though, had a flat head like that. I later described it to the old-timers around town, but none of them had ever seen anything like it. I sometimes wonder if I just thought the head was that of a rattler when it really wasn't, that maybe I panicked a bit when I first saw it, as hard as that is to believe.

I repaired about a mile's worth of barbwire fencing around the place, replacing broken cedar posts with metal ones, about the same time we decided to revive the Pony Express. The Pony Express had run from St. Joseph, Missouri, to Sacramento, California, for eighteen months in 1860–1861, and its route had brought it through the Toiyabe Mountains three miles north of Austin. One afternoon, having driven into town for goodies, we were sitting in the restaurant with a kid named Mike Pellagatti—a nut who, like us, hung around with Joe Dory and the associated wild bunch—when he and Marlys came up with the idea of reenacting the Pony Express from Austin to Carson City. The plan was to do it over the Fourth of July holiday. We could recruit a bunch of riders, outfit ourselves in buckskin, sell letters "carried by Pony Express," and become rich and famous overnight, no doubt about it.

"Well, OK," I said, doubtfully, "but I'm gonna need a horse." I didn't think riding itself would be a problem for me. Although I hadn't been on a horse in years and years, I had grown up around them and had ridden a lot as a kid. My father even left me his saddle, an old Porter 37, which I still had, plus a bridle and horse blanket and spurs and chaps and everything else you might even remotely need to ride off into the sunset. Except, of course, the horse.

In the manner of all things Austin, Cindy Jolly happened to be sitting in the booth across from us, listening to all this, and said, "I have a horse you can use." So there it was. I had the gear and the horse and, with the newly repaired fence at Lynch Creek, a place to put the horse and practice riding.

We called ourselves the Pony Express Second Edition, ignorant as we were that an association yearly runs the entire route from St. Joseph to Sacramento. Had we found that out, after getting ourselves all worked up, I imagine we would have gone ahead and run it anyway; a good idea doesn't become any less good just because everybody and his brother are doing it.

We needed publicity to sell letters, so we notified area newspapers and TV stations, and we set up a demonstration run at what was then the 102 Ranch, just off Interstate 80 a few miles east of Reno. I got bucked off while relaying the saddlebags, but it never made the evening news because the ABC cameraman, a novice named Tad Dunbar, was busy falling into an irrigation ditch while I was doing a half-gainer off the horse. Hmm. Perhaps this wasn't going to be all that easy.

But we pulled it off. With help from a lot of folks around Austin, and riders from five different states, and their horses and horse trailers and collateral gear, and tack and hay and oats and water, and tents and motor homes and folding chairs and sunscreen, we managed to do what a dozen station managers and riders with captured mustangs did a century before. It was fun all right, but man, was it a lot of work.

When it was all over, Cindy let me keep her horse, Flecka, at Lynch Creek the remainder of the summer. That's where I really started to enjoy riding again, and Flecka and I explored all the canyons and half the nearby mountains. There's something timeless about riding a horse through sagebrush country. It's an unhurried, measured existence that gives full awareness to your senses—sight, sound, motion, they sink in all the way to your core. I don't believe there's any more effective way of living in the present moment than on horseback.

Lynch Creek offered an idyllic life that we never tired of, probably because we didn't live it long enough. (I imagine if you spent a winter up there you'd be chewing the linoleum and frothing at the mouth.) As much as we loved it, though, we had to leave early. It was a drought year, and the spring that fed the creek dried up in mid-September. You can live without a lot of things—electricity, phones, neighbors—but you cannot live without water. Even the pond dried up, leaving my raft lying askew on cracked alkali. The day we pulled out of Lynch Creek was a sad day, indeed.

And coming back into Austin was a sad day. The luster, that wonderful feeling of finally having found what you'd been looking for all of your life, had worn off, as I believe it does for everybody who puts all their eggs in a happiness-is-a-place basket. Again leaving the restaurant in the hands of Harry and Linda, Marlys and I moved to Nampa, Idaho, because we were fed up with the whole central Nevada experience. We rented a small house, and I went to work welding fifth-wheel trailers together for a manufacturing company near Boise. Now we were cooking, by golly. Driving to work in the morning, though, felt uncomfortably like driving to work in California, except now I had snow to contend with. Also with traffic and stoplights and lines at the bank. It didn't take to long to wake up to the fact that we'd somehow managed to make ourselves worse off than ever before. Three months was all it took. We went back to the Stagecoach Inn as quickly as we could pack our stuff and move out, this time wide awake and with no fairy-tale endings clouding our minds.

Coming back to Austin felt like coming home, which was a first for me because I'd lived in a dozen different towns growing up and never really had what I considered a home. It was a revelation that sticks with me to this day. I had a *real home.* Nothing ever felt better.

Unless maybe it was chukar hunting.

Chukar partridge are categorized as upland game birds, as opposed to migratory birds. They're bigger than quail, with a body about the size of a brick, and if need be they can drop out of your sights like one. They are gray-brown with distinctive black diagonal stripes running down their sides, and appear to be wearing black ninja masks across their eyes. They are not native to Nevada or, for that matter, to the United States. They were introduced from India in the 1890s to Midwest cornfields where food was abundant and the terrain was flat and friendly. The fact that chukar didn't do at all well in that environment, that they thrive only in rocky, barren desert country such as that found in the Great Basin, should tell you all you need to know about the bird. It should also tell you a bit about the hunters who pursue him.

It takes a well-placed shotgun pattern to bring a chukar partridge out of the sky, and the work isn't done even then because you have to find it. I discovered early on that you don't want to take your eyes off of the spot where the bird hit the ground, not only because chukar blend into the desert so well, but because they are often able to run several yards after being brought down. When that happens you really need to know exactly where they started from. Sometimes, especially if there's a skiff of snow on the ground, you can track them. Otherwise you have to crawl around and look beneath each and every sagebrush in an ever-expanding circle until you find them, like Elmer Fudd searching for that darned wabbit.

I was introduced to shotgunning in general and chukar hunting in particular by Joe Ramos. I saw him shooting at clay pigeons with a shotgun down near the rodeo grounds, and my curiosity got the best of me. He had a little metal gizmo that threw the clays, which look like miniature ceramic flying saucers, out and away at great speed, whereupon he'd shoulder his gun and blast the clay into a puff of black dust. He was having the devil of a time trying to do everything by himself, though, and he needed someone to work the thrower, which is where I came in. Working the thrower, or some derivative thereof, was where I always seemed to come in, but it was fun and resulted in me trying my hand at the shooting end of it.

It looked easy enough, as I'd grown up around rifles and even earned a rifle expert badge in the Marine Corps. However, a shotgun is not a rifle, a fact that I quickly came to appreciate. For one thing the recoil of a 12-gauge shotgun is easily twice that of any rifle I've ever fired, so you really need to lean hard into it before pulling the trigger. And whereas you might occasionally get away with snapping off a quick shot before firmly seating a rifle to your shoulder, you don't even want to think about it with a shotgun.

From a rifleman's point of view, though, the oddest thing about a shotgun is the lack of a recognizable rear sight and therefore the lack of an obvious way to line up on the target, which is moving too fast to get a clean bead on anyway. I missed four successive clays, not quite separating my shoulder from the rest of me, before I conceded that I could use some tutoring. Man, it was like learning something new. After I got the hang of it I bought my own Remington Model 870 shotgun, and it was an easy step from there into the world of chukar hunting.When the season opened that year Ramos took me to Italian Canyon, eight miles north of Austin, where we knocked the heck out of them. I was hooked, but unbeknownst to me there are two kinds of chukar: opening-day chukar, who are dumber than dirt and fly up at the perfect distance in perfect target formation, and educated chukar, survivors who have seen the business end of a shotgun and who thereafter turn into the birdie equivalent of First Force Recon. They post sentries, they send out decoys, and they run uphill before they break cover somewhere near the top, then turn and fly back down.

The second time we went out Ramos took me to a place he called Chukar Heaven, so called, he claimed, because of the cornucopia abundance of partridges that you had to kick out of the way to get a good shot at one. Initially he was right. Chukar scattered everywhere as we drove up to the base of the ridge, apparently leaving a vacuum, which, in compliance with the laws of nature, fools then rush in to fill. On this day that would be Ramos, me, and his dog Jack. Jack was supposed to be a bird dog, which he probably was as he didn't look all that bright, and he took after the chukar for all he was worth in about twenty different directions. Because of his frantic looping he never got very far away and Joe was able to bring him under control relatively quickly. That didn't last long. The birds didn't want to fly, and wouldn't unless you stepped on them, which drove poor old Jack absolutely bonkers. Ramos finally had to chain him to the bumper of his pickup to keep the poor little guy from having a nervous breakdown. It would have been merciful had he chained me there, too.

We started weaving our way up the hill toward the ridge, and it was obvious we were driving a fairly large group, or herd, or pride, of chukar because we could hear them chukking away, and now and then we'd catch a flash of feathers between the sagebrush. As we neared the top it became evident that we'd been duped, as one lone decoy, who'd been chukking away madly, broke hard to the right and flew past me back down the hill before I could even shoulder my gun. Ramos said he was afraid that would happen, that the main bunch, or school, or pod, of chukar would sneak off unnoticed while the one who drew the short straw took us on a wild goose—so to speak—chase.

The wily partridges gave us one more chance, as they regrouped at the bottom and swung around for another performance. We fell for it again, and even though we were watching carefully, neither one of us saw where they split up, or where they went. Enough is enough, so we loaded up Jack and left. Before we got out of the canyon Ramos pointed at a rock about a third of the way up the hill on our right. The rock looked like it had a bottle sitting on top of it, but Ramos said it was a chukar standing sentry duty for the rest of the group, or pack, or horde. Hmm. "Ahem" was the best I could do, but he handed me a pair of binoculars, and sure enough, a chukar was standing on top of that rock, apparently at parade rest.

"Ahem ahem ahem," I said and handed the binoculars back.

Ramos circled to the right while I went straight up the hill, hoping to drive them in his direction. I looked down at my footing once, and when I looked back up the sentry was gone. I heard some chukking beyond the rock, but having been recently educated I turned around and went back to the truck, where Jack and I waited until Ramos returned. When he came back he was carrying two chukar, although I hadn't heard any shots. I guess that shouldn't have been surprising, though, as Jack and I had been listening to golden oldies on the radio, the most recent of which had been "Mockingbird Hill," tra-la-la twiddlee-dee-dee. Those were the last chukar I saw for the rest of the season. You can go crazy, being treated like that by a bird, and I think maybe I did the next few years. Chukar season runs roughly from October into January, and during those months, if I wasn't working I was out hunting chukar. My nickname, thanks to Ramos, even became "Chukar," which took a long time to die out after I gave up hunting. It's still my name, as far as Joe is concerned.

Deer hunting is generally good in the whole state of Nevada, but you do have to put your name in for a random drawing in order to get a tag. I tried perhaps four or five times without any success and eventually just gave up on deer hunting altogether, although I was never very enthusiastic about it anyway; there's a lot of work involved in bagging large animals, and even more after the bagging is done. I may try to draw a deer tag again, but you know, birds are small, and they're a lot easier to prepare, so I may not, too.

Fishing is good in central Nevada, but it's a different kind of fishing then I ever experienced. Before moving to Austin I'd fished in Washington, Oregon, and California, and trout fishing in those states is enhanced by spincasting, where you can throw the bait as far from the bank as possible. That way, you don't have to worry about the wily trout glimpsing either you or your shadow, so you don't have to sneak up on them like you do here. The streams around Austin, taking into account the upper Reese River country, number maybe a dozen or so, and every single one of them is, in fisherman terms, dinky. You can step across them, although you might have to walk a little to find a narrow enough place in the springtime, and the water depth seldom exceeds a foot or two. Most are planted with rainbow trout by the state Department of Wildlife, and those are what you mostly catch. There are native brook and German trout in there too, but most fishermen aren't up to the challenge of getting one of those because the big lunkers hang out in the brushiest, most tackle-stealing pockets you can imagine, such as beaver dams. I usually give wide berth to those places on my way upstream to catch some pan-size rainbow.

For an easier day of fishing there is Groves Lake, thirty miles south of Austin on the Smoky Valley side of the Toiyabe Mountains. Kingston Creek feeds Groves Lake with snowmelt and springwater and trout, although the lake, too, is planted. The first time I fished Groves Lake, I caught an eighteen-inch rainbow. Outwitted him, by George. I threw my line out with a bobber fastened ten feet above the hook, which was festooned with red salmon eggs, propped my pole against a forked willow stick, and leaned back against the bank. Mr. Wily Trout wasn't expecting that, any of it, and within an hour or two he fell for it. Happily, the clattering of the pole against the rocks woke me in time to grab it while the reel was still above the waterline, and I brought my trophy fish to shore with a display of angling skill that was just short of inspiring, if I do say so myself. After I landed it a couple of nearby fishermen said it was a fluke, but I know a trout when I see one.

Kingston Creek above Groves Lake winds through several meadows and offers good angling all the way up. A dirt road runs alongside the creek to its headwaters, then climbs over a mountain saddle and drops down to Big Creek, twelve miles south of Austin, on the west flank of the Toiyabes. You can also find good stream fishing below Groves Lake all the way to the mouth of the canyon, and although most of the canyon is too narrow to pull off and camp, there is a Forest Service campground two miles below the lake. The small community of Kingston, complete with a lodge, a church, and a general store, fans out from the mouth of the canyon.

Birch Creek, easily accessible from State Route 376 three miles south of Highway 50, is one of those brushy streams that take a lot of patience to fish, but it will reward a persistent angler. There are undeveloped campsites at the mouth of the canyon, but as with Kingston Creek, camping beyond that point is limited by to the narrowness of the canyon. The road fords the creek in several places as it winds upward, and in the summertime you can generally travel over the top of the mountains and down into Austin by two-wheel drive, *if* your vehicle has enough ground clearance to keep from getting hung up at the rocky crossings.

Nevada has also been blessed with several hot springs, many of which have been developed into spas in more populated areas of the state. Other springs in the backcountry are undeveloped and much less known. Spencer's Hot Springs bubbles out of the ground in the foothills of the Toquima Mountains twenty miles east of Austin. To get there, take State Route 376 south from Highway 50 and then turn left at the first dirt road, about a half mile south of the junction. Five miles out, when you reach the power lines, turn left. The road winds around a bit, and after about a mile and a half you'll see roads branching off and heading every which way. Stay on the one that goes straight ahead, mostly, and follow it to the top of the hill. You'll see a small wooden platform to your left on a slight rise, and that's where the main pool is—there are others, if you care to explore. Check the temperature of the water before getting in, as the water coming out of the springs may be scalding; you can adjust the flow into the pond to cool it off. *Caution: Watching a desert sunset while soaking in Spencer's Hot Springs can be addictive, and may cause loss of stress.*

Back in the 1960s the citizens of Austin got together and, in a classic effort of teamwork and cooperation, built an Olympic-size swimming pool at Spencer's. They somehow made it out of poured concrete, which had to be a difficult chore at best out there in the middle of the desert. Then they constructed wooden changing rooms, complete with roofing and doors. When I moved to Austin in 1974 all this was still there, and I thought it one of the modern marvels of the world; imagine going for a swim in a regular swimming pool, at the base of a remote mountain range in the Great Basin Desert, without another soul in sight. At the time the area was also a favorite haunt of wild burros, and there were several faded wooden buildings left from an old tungsten mining operation. I half expected Rod Serling to walk out of the sagebrush and welcome us to the latest episode of *The Twilight Zone*.

It couldn't last, of course. Someone drowned in the pool, and the liability of having a swimming pool without lifeguards on government land prompted the Bureau of Land Management to bulldoze it into oblivion. You can still find little pieces of concrete around the area, all that is left of the darndest swimming pool I ever saw. The old mine buildings are gone now too, said to have been burned to the ground by biker gangs in a party mood. And the burros? Some were found shot, and the rest just disappeared. And that, as Forrest Gump might say, is all I have to say about Spencer's Hot Springs.

This country is so vast and so open that it's hard to find something you *can't* do. I took up riding motorcycles—the kind with the knobby tires that will go just about anywhere you have the nerve to aim them—with my much younger brother-in-law, Robbie. For three summers we rode down every goat path we could find, and some we couldn't. The problem I had was remembering that a two-wheeled dirt bike is not a four-wheeled tour bus, and my gawking around caused several mishaps that debiked me in very creative and inelegant ways. One of these incidents, caused by inadvertently running into a patch of sand at 50 MPH, made such an impression on me, and the surrounding desert, that I sold my motorcycle in the hope of eventually healing up.

The sport of mountain biking—the kind without engines—is growing in popularity around Austin at this time, although I don't practice it myself. The T-Rix Mountain Bike shop, working in conjunction with the Chamber of Commerce and the Forest Service, has mapped out several maintained and marked bike trails that cover some of the most spectacular scenery in the area. They hold annual races in the late summer months, and although Austin doesn't have a lot of motel rooms available, you can camp just about anywhere. Having ridden motorcycles up and down these hills, I find it hard to believe people pedal bicycles along the same routes. Tires me out watching them, I can tell you. These days, I'd just as soon sit out on the deck with a frosty glass of ice tea.

So I do.

KIDS

When I moved to Austin the furthest thing from my mind was kids. I didn't have any of my own, and although Marlys had three, they were all out of high school. Therefore I didn't pay any attention to the schools or to any activities that might be kid-oriented. However, I couldn't help but notice that the kids around Austin were, wonder of wonders, polite. There were still remnants of respect and selflessness left in the kids where we came from, but even those bits and pieces seemed to be fading. That's not to say there wasn't any mischievousness around my new home, but I saw no intentional meanness, and there is a big difference. Gangs and drugs and graffiti, which were beginning to rear their ugly heads in Antioch, were noticeably absent in Austin.

There were other things, though. The day before Halloween in our first autumn here, I was sitting on one of the benches in front of our ice cream parlor when Carol, who owned the business next to ours, came out and started wrestling with a heavy antique bench grinder that she kept in front of her store. I went over and helped, naturally, but was curious as to why she wanted to put the grinder inside her store all of a sudden.

"The night before Halloween is Gate Night," she said, as if that explained something. Then she pointed at our sidewalk benches and added, "You might want to put those inside too, while you've still got them."

I smiled and thanked her, then went back to sitting in the autumn sunshine on the very benches she thought might escape. This was Austin, for goodness sake, not Los Angeles. I wasn't putting bars on my windows and I wasn't putting my benches inside, thank you. I hadn't thought of Carol as paranoid, so her comment was a little disquieting, but there was no doubt in my mind that my benches would still be there in the morning.

In the morning my benches were gone. I found them quickly enough; they were positioned neatly on the centerline of Highway 50 along with trash cans, wheelbarrows, appliances, bicycles, and nearly every other portable item in southern Lander County, including a couple of old wooden outhouses, the whole collection stretching from one end of town to the other. Ahh, I thought, Gate Night.

It apparently began a century ago with, well, gates, which were quietly removed from their hinges in the middle of the night before Halloween and then propped up down the center of Main Street. The modern version had little to do with gates, as there were easier pickings all over town, like my benches. Older kids were the perpetrators of Gate Night. Small kids were confined to ordinary Halloween trick-or-treating, but as they grew up they were indoctrinated into the ways of their elders—sort of like Indians, but not. The tradition had been handed down, generation to generation, each one trying to outdo the one before, until it had become downright hazardous. The dump over in Slaughterhouse Canyon, unattended and full to the brim with castoff items such as old refrigerators, would be dang near empty on Halloween morning. The state Highway Department cleaned up quickly, loading the errant objects onto dump trucks and hauling them off before the traffic picked up. If you had benches on the centerline you'd better be up at dawn to retrieve them, before the highway crew got there.

In 1981, after several years of near catastrophes involving drivers startled witless by outhouses in their headlights, the newly elected sheriff officially outlawed Gate Night and told his newly hired Austin deputy to enforce it.

Knowing the futility of trying to outwit kids in their cars, the deputy sat motionless and, hopefully, inconspicuous in his patrol unit in front of the sheriff's office, where he could observe a good portion of Main Street centerline and also several side streets layered up the hillside across the highway. He saw absolutely nothing—no kids, no cars, no movement—and by and by he became convinced that the sheriff's warning had been taken to heart. Of course, the deputy couldn't see beyond the state yard to his right where the highway curved behind a hill, and where the centerline was quickly masked by axles and stoves and garbage cans, nor could he see beyond the Chevron station to his left, where shadowy figures were putting the finishing touches on a wall of appliances, cinder blocks, and milk crates. The shadowy figures were confident they could finish the stretch in between once the deputy found he'd been duped and shifted his efforts into trying to chase them down. And that is exactly what happened. I know, because I was that deputy.

Despite ongoing law enforcement efforts, Gate Night never was shut down by force of will, but it did die out naturally, in its own time and of its own accord, a few years later. Thank goodness, for the most part—but still it is strangely sad to see old traditions, even hazardous ones, fade.

When the mines opened up in the early 1980s many families moved into both Austin and the Kingston–Gillman Springs area. Most were good people whose breadwinners made their livings by following mining companies from boom to boom, much like military families who transfer from base to base. A few were not. Those few were generally unsavory, and because the apple does indeed fall close to the tree, their children were often cheerless and cruel as well, and introduced illegal drugs to school, along with the associated ills of burglary and vandalism. The sheriff's office put on a fourth deputy and increased the number of reservists in hopes of stemming the increase in crime.

The school, a two-story brick structure built in the late 1920s, became overcrowded to the point that a separate high school was built a mile north of town just off the Battle Mountain highway. As soon as that school was completed, of course, the price of gold dropped low enough that the mining boom ended as suddenly as it began, and the population of Austin started declining again. Once started, illegal drugs don't die out as easily, and I don't believe Austin has ever been drug-free since, although they've never resurfaced as a major problem.

The sheriff's office was able to return to a three-deputy schedule and released most of the reservists after the mines closed, thereby putting its official stamp on Austin's return to normal. However, now there were two schools: the old elementary school in the heart of town and the new high school outside town. There were now also two gymnasiums, and sports, which have always held center stage throughout the school year, became consistently available to elementary kids for the first time. The Austin Broncos and the Austin Fillies now had farm teams coming up in the Austin Colts and the Junior Fillies. It was a great time to be a parent in Austin, I would think so, anyway; I wasn't yet a parent.

When Val and I married in 1986, she had two sons, Josh, eleven, and Jed, nine. To my undying regret I never really got involved with them until they were no longer children, by which time we'd all missed out on a lot of neat stuff. My focus was on our daughter, Withanee, born in August of 1987. It was then that I came to fully appreciate Austin. Val's parents lived just down the hill from us, and so did her sister and brother-in-law. Withanee and her brothers had relatives and cousins all over the place and numerous friends who were just like cousins, and that gave us a lot of peace of mind. It was virtually impossible for anything to happen without a protector being right there. When Withanee started school, in the building where Val taught fifth grade, I often watched her walk down the hill into the playground, which was just across Sixth Street at the base of the hill. As the years went by, the walk became easier for her, and I watched her grow up walking down that hill, from barely being able to keep upright in the snowdrifts to hopping around them to striding through them, all the while hanging onto her books and looking around at the world like it was a new and wondrous thing. Because of her I was once again blessed with that same view, and those were wonderful years indeed.

While a good education is important, it isn't all there is to childhood or even the most significant part, for that matter. I don't know about anybody else, but I remember very little about what went on in school when I was a kid. It was like holding a job for us little people, but we didn't get paid. No, my childhood is best remembered for running barefoot in the summer, and learning to roller skate, and riding a bicycle with no hands, and seeing who could walk on the highest stilts. I'm not sure why open country is so much more beneficial to childhood than cinder block and asphalt, but from my experience it undeniably is, and from that perspective Austin was the perfect place to grow up. Within a hundred feet of our house we had hillsides to sled down in winter, trees to climb in summer, a lawn from which to watch the clouds or run through sprinklers, an immense open area for treasure hunts and Easter eggs, a dirt bank that was great for digging and shooting BB guns, a basketball net, a trampoline, horseshoe pits, a playhouse accessed by a yellow brick road, and birdbaths and butterflies and ladybugs and even, occasionally, mud puddles. It doesn't get much better than that, even for us adults.

We built a deck and a brick barbecue overlooking the valley, and Withanee often had her friends over in the summertime, which was the only excuse we needed to barbecue hot dogs and cheeseburgers. Before too long Val's parents, Ron and Terry Gandolfo, would join us, along with Val's sister, Michelle, and Michelle's husband, Rob. All of them lived on our hill, and all had a large part in raising Withanee from the very start, so in those informal gatherings, never was heard a discouraging word and the skies were not cloudy all day. On those days we were, without doubt, home on the range.

Josh and Jed were both in the Boy Scouts, and Withanee followed in the Girl Scout program. To get her Compass merit badge she had to attend a day camp in Eureka, seventy miles east of Austin, so Val and I drove her. The instructors allowed us accompany her on the course and even help her out now and then if she got confused. Since I'd been a Cub Scout, a Boy Scout, a Sea Scout, and a U.S. Marine, I offered my help, but I somehow got us a little turned around. Withanee was able to recover in time to earn her merit badge, and she never told anybody about her woodsman dad, for which I'm still grateful. Val and I were even invited to join With in tie-dying our own T-shirts afterward, and I have mine to this day. It's really neat, with this big yellow and red sunburst in the middle. I've never once become lost while wearing it.

As a Girl Scout, Withanee also got me hooked on the caramel cookies they sell every year. I'd bought Girl Scout cookies ever since I was old enough to have my own money, but I never really appreciated them until I started driving Withanee around town with her portable cookie market. I'd always favored the peanut butter or mint cookies, but she persuaded me to try caramel, and that was all it took for our cabinets at home to be overstocked with crates of the things. You know, just in case civilization collapses before the next cookie sale. We also ordered cookies from the other

Girl Scouts in her troop whenever we were approached, in order to spread the revenue around, and since neither Val nor I knew what the other was doing we usually ended up with enough cookies to feed Val's school class for a month, which I believe happened a couple of times.

Some of the kids who attended school in Austin lived out on ranches and were bused in every day. Ashley Young, a classmate of Withanee's whose family lived at the Birch Creek Ranch in Smoky Valley, would invite her out for the day, or even a weekend, now and then, and Withanee got to see what life on a ranch was like. The kids rode both pivot sprinklers and horses, and climbed around on tractors, and played fox-and-hound with swivel sprinklers, and although the equipment may have differed from that of a century ago, the lifestyle hadn't changed much. The kids still had chores, and the adults still worked long and hard haying and taking care of their livestock, and the family unit was still the glue that held the ranch together.

Our daughter also took part in the new elementary school basketball program, which was a real hoot. These guys were little, and I mean *little*, when you compared them with the size of the basketball, and the court, and even their uniforms. There were elementary teams in Eureka and Round Mountain, as they also had spare gyms that weren't in use by high schools, and we were treated to some great games. By "we" I mean the spectators. The kids mostly looked confused. It was a terrific introduction to team sports for them, though, and it was really nice that the smaller kids had an inside activity for the winter months.

Sometime around the sixth grade, Austin students become active in school fundraisers. The biggest of these is the annual Big Creek Run, which takes place at the end of September. The run is open to both students and ambitious adults who, in a fit of optimism, sign up to run the twelve miles from the mouth of Big Creek to the rodeo grounds below Austin. Participants then go around to everybody they can think of and ask for pledges based on how many miles they successfully complete. The pledges, which usually run anywhere from a nickel to a couple of dollars per mile, are payable at the end of the run and are used to finance high school sports costs associated with away trips. It is considered bad form to drop out for any but medical reasons, so there is a lot of gasping and wheezing among the older contestants along the route, and even some among the kids. The Big Creek Run is always scheduled on a weekday, and students who participate get one final day out of the classroom before cold weather sets in. A bus takes the kids out early in the morning and drops them off at the starting line near the mouth of the canyon, which could easily be the loneliest starting line in America. Water stops are placed two miles from the start and every mile thereafter, manned by volunteers who often dispense snacks and encouragement along with paper cups of water.

My daughter ran every Big Creek event from 1999 to 2006, and I helped out with water stops as often as I could. Manning a water stop on an early autumn day in the desert is among the most enjoyable things you can find to do with your time, as far as I'm concerned, because the weather is almost always pleasant and crystal clear. I'd generally get to my assigned mile marker before the bus even left the school, find the best view to set up a folding chair, and slip into a coma. You could see the runners coming ten or fifteen minutes before they arrived, which usually gave me enough time to get to my feet and have cups of water ready to hand out. I'd also have some cookies ready, or perhaps slice up some apples if I happened upon a burst of energy, and no matter where I was stationed, I'd remind the runners that it was downhill from there on out, which, of course, it wasn't. Still, they always seemed grateful for the thought. Then I'd rest up for the next batch.

In 2004, when Withanee was a junior, I happened to be assigned mile ten, two miles from the finish line. It was a warm day, and With and some of her classmates wanted to inflict water damage upon their high school science teacher, Bill Cox, who was manning the final water stop at mile eleven. Normally I wouldn't be caught dead plotting against a teacher, but this would be in retaliation for a dousing my daughter and her friends had taken the year before, and since Bill was my golf partner, I made an exception. I hid some loaded Super-Soaker squirt guns and water balloons beneath a sagebrush about hundred feet from Bill's location and gave With and her buddies a map as they went by. They found the goods and had an enjoyable ambush, I was told, but the map fell into Bill's hands, and from it he was able to identify me. He accused me of being an arms merchant, and to this day he informs anybody who happens to be around of my sleazy nature. He also flipped a couple of water balloons at my water stop as he drove by the following year, and I had to watch out for him thereafter, which severely cut into my coma time.

Other fundraising activities are conducted by each class as they come up through high school: bake sales, raffles, dances, rec nights, community dinners, town team tournaments, car washes, and holiday-specific sales of items like Christmas wreaths and Valentine candy. When you also factor in unfunded programs such as Close Up, which yearly sends seniors on a week-long trip to Washington, DC, and donations for summer sports camps for our volleyball and basketball teams, the funds that are raised in this end of the county for our students are staggering. It is the ongoing individual selflessness of everybody in the community that makes it happen each and every year, and it demonstrates the strength of character present in rural America.

The building that was once Austin's fire station in the days of horse-drawn fire wagons, and is still topped by the alarm bell tower, continues its community service today as Austin's youth center. It is located on the corner of Main and Cedar streets and is staffed by volunteers who keep it open in the evenings, giving the kids a place to play pool or video games or just hang out. Also, in the summertime the Bert T. Gandolfo Park on the upper end of town provides a swimming pool, picnic area, and ball field. The park is also equipped with a supersized barbecue pit that is used for special events throughout the season. Most of the kids in this part of central Nevada learned to swim in the pool, which is open from June to September as weather permits. The lifeguards are employed by Lander County and are mainly those very same kids who went on to get their lifeguard certification, my daughter among them. What a terrific summer job in the Great Basin Desert, huh?

One of the fundraising events put on for Close Up last summer was a softball tournament at the park. Withanee organized both the event and one of the teams, on which I played catcher. My advice to other parents would be: Don't try to play baseball with kids unless you're either (a) in terrific shape, or (b) not very bright. It hurts. For days.

When it comes to passive entertainment, the only movie theater Austin ever had was in the building that now houses the Owl Club Bar on Main Street. You still walk up the ramp that used to lead to theater seats, although they've been replaced with bar stools. The nearest movie theater now is in Fallon, 112 miles away, and the nearest multiplex theaters are in Reno. Therefore going to a movie is still a treat for Austin kids, which makes both the movies and the kids a lot more fun. And television, well, until satellite TV came to town with the small dishes, around 1994, most kids in this end of the county—shoot, most adults, too—were limited to the three major networks, and then only part of the time. It was rare indeed when all three were functional at the same time, and the pictures were, as a rule, awful. Nobody wants to go back to the way it was, but there were advantages to life before we all had two hundred crystal-clear channels, even in the winter, even in the Great Basin Desert.

As it is with movies, so it is with other city attractions. The malls, for instance: Our kids get a real bang out of going shopping simply because there isn't any around here to speak of. I never did like to shop, but after a month or two, even I kind of enjoy the big stores and the stocked shelves. I've noticed that Reno malls are packed with kids after school hours, not just hanging out but walking through the corridors with purposeful strides, as if they knew exactly where they were going. Do they? We Austinites sure don't, and we usually have the map boards all to ourselves, trying to figure out where, precisely, the You Are Here arrow is in relation to our parking space.

A wonderful benefit of small-town schools with small student populations is that every single student has the opportunity to take an active part in everything that goes on, from stage plays to sports. It seems they all start by performing in the elementary school Christmas program, which is traditionally attended by the entire community. Some productions get pretty elaborate, with plays like *A Sombrero for Santa* weaving singing and dancing throughout the story line in the manner of a Broadway show. You ain't lived till you've seen a line of first-graders, draped in serapes and wearing sombreros, playing "Jingle Bells" on ukuleles. Sadly, with the recent closure of the old school, along with its gymnasium, the elementary Christmas program has become a watered-down shadow of its former self at the new school, sandwiched between junior high and high school holiday skits. Although those aren't bad, either.

Once a student enters high school, there is the occasional stage play. Withanee landed the part of Mary Christmas in the 2001 production of *Mistletoe Mesa* and was the choreographer for *Through the Looking Glass,* a musical performed by the junior high grades. She's sung numerous solos and participated in complex—to me, anyway—dance routines, and so have all the other students. I think that certainly gives them a leg up when they go on to bigger and better things, because they already know how to cope with the primal fear that grips us when called upon to make some sort of public presentation, whether in college or the workday world.

Sports in Nevada high schools are divided into leagues that are labeled 1A, for the smallest student populations, through 4A, for the largest. The idea is to separate the schools that have from those that have not, so that athletes from Reno, handpicked from among the hundreds who tried out for the team, aren't going against athletes who've been shanghaied in order to fill out the roster, as we often do in Austin. In 2003 there were only six girls in high school who were able to play varsity volleyball. Since a volleyball team requires six players, there was some discussion as to whether they should even field a team. Val, my wife, was the coach, and they all sat down before the first practice to decide whether they even wanted to try, with the result that all six, plus the coach, committed themselves not only to playing, but to finishing the entire season. Further stacking the odds against them was the lack of varsity experience; two were sophomores, including my daughter, and the other four were freshman. The silver lining was that because they were so few, they didn't need to travel to away games in a school bus, so I became their driver in a twelve-passenger school van, and we were like one big happy family motoring down the highway.

It didn't take long for word to travel around the state, and the smallest team competing in varsity volleyball became known as the "Iron Six." Every girl played every game, no matter the inevitable illness or injury that plagues all athletes. They played through a debilitating flu season, and they played with sprained ankles and jammed fingers and the exhaustion that sets in at the sixth game of a doubleheader, and Val used her time-outs only when someone needed to be taped up or the team had to catch their collective breath. They didn't just stumble through the season either; they fought every game to the very end and finished the season with a 14-4 record, earning a second-seed place in the regional tournament. They lost in the first round to a California team from Coleville—as far as the score goes, anyway. In our minds there wasn't a loser among them, and it remains my greatest honor to have been affiliated with the Iron Six.

Basketball starts soon after volleyball ends, and the girls' team is usually the volleyball team with different uniforms. Injuries such as sprains, which don't heal quickly, are carried from one sport to the other with the hopes that "it'll get better." Since there are only five people on a basketball team, there's at least some chance of sitting out, but more often the injured player just grits her teeth and goes. Basketball, of course, requires a different set of skills that use different muscles, so it's a large change from volleyball. The advantage for the girls is that they're already used to working as a team. The boys' team has to start from scratch and usually gets off to a slower start.

Whether it's the boys' team or the girls,' basketball, for most Austin residents, is *the* sport. Many former players are among the fans. Val's father, Ron, played on the 1954 Bronco team that won the state title, the trophy for which still sits proudly in the school's display case, along with the autographed ball from the title game. So do what seems like an awful lot of trophies for a school the size of Austin's; there is very little space left over for the future in a cabinet that covers one entire wall of the high school.

The only other sports offered in Austin are track-and-field and cross-country, both of which are almost always away events for us. Cross-country running isn't a very good spectator sport because you can only glimpse a small part of the course, and since its season coincides with volleyball season I've never attended any of the meets, although Austin has had respectable showings over the years. Track starts in March, which seems a little early in this part of the country. We often have snow into May, and extremely cold track meets are the norm for a good part of the season. However, the kids don't seem to mind the cold nearly as much as their parents do. I've attended track meets that would keep polar bears indoors, but it doesn't slow the athletes down at all. Nothing seems to. In contrast, the Nevada state championships were held in Las Vegas in 2005, after a particularly cold track season when the temperature was seldom above 45 degrees, and our girls' relay team took third place even though the thermometer at race time soared to 105, twice as hot as anyplace they'd ever run.

Of everything that affects children growing up in Austin, I'm convinced the most beneficial is the physical nearness of family members. It sounds dopey, but Austin's compact layout is the perfect solution to the thorny child-rearing problems that result from spreading kajillions of people over huge areas. In Austin we can easily find out where our kids are, who they're with, and what they're doing, not because we're ace detectives, but because there's no place for them to hide. Austin isn't a concentration camp; kids still sneak out at night, and they still test parental limits, and they still rebel when they feel they're being treated unfairly. But we can easily find out what they're up to, which makes parenting a lot easier, at least when it comes to the real world. The real and present danger to our kids today is the virtual world, the thing that can't be overcome by our remoteness, in the form of the Internet.

It has been said that the Internet is a tool and has no inherent powers of its own, which may be—probably is—true. There is so much information available, information that remote areas such as Austin wouldn't otherwise have access to, that the Internet has become invaluable in a relatively short time. So short that us old folks haven't had the time, or the knowledge, to help our kids stay away from the electronic quicksand that has already become a threat to their very existence. If there are safeguards, they are too slow in getting here. The world has shrunk, finally, to the point where Austin and its sister towns no longer have the built-in protection they've always had for their kids. The Internet has done to Austin what air travel did to the United States: eliminated the safety that was offered by moats, whether they be in the form of oceans or of deserts.

Still, our kids have a sense of the real world, the dirt and the bugs and the creatures and the clouds and the stars, that isn't present in the city. They have a working knowledge of nature, not one that is conjured up through a window in Washington, DC, or invented by activists in San Francisco, and the kids raised out here next to the ground are quite likely the best hope we'll ever have that common sense will prevail in America.

After being around these kids for the past three decades, I see our future as looking a lot brighter than I once thought was possible.

THE VIEW

In the end, the most compelling reason to move to high desert country is the view. No matter where you stand in central Nevada—weather
permitting, of course—you can see blue sky and distant mountain ranges.
Everything in between is God's bonus, and it is always different. There is a
one-mile stretch of Austin's Main Street that, because it runs along the canyon bottom, offers a restricted view. This is where the business district is
located, though, and because of the historical distractions you don't really
notice the lack of openness.

I was working in the Stagecoach Inn many years ago when an English
couple came in for lunch. They had flown over from London, where they
lived, and had rented a car in San Francisco with the intention of driving
across America. The husband was trying to soothe his wife, who was vis-
ibly shaken. He told me she'd ridden the last hundred miles hunched over
beneath the dashboard so she couldn't see out the windows. The country
was too big for her, he said, and the very enormousness of it made her
disoriented and dizzy. The lady nodded at that and added, "It's so . . . so
vahst!" Vahst? Oh, vast. She felt a lot better now that they were hemmed in,
as it were, by the friendly confines of Main Street.

As you move up the hillsides, though, the canyon widens to reveal the
Reese River Valley far below, and the distant Shoshone Mountains stretch
like a fence across the western horizon. The valley floor can appear as flat
as a billiard table or as undulating as ocean swells, depending on the shad-
ing. And the lady from England got it right; it is *vahst!*

When Val and I married, we had a double-wide manufactured home—or trailer house, to the less sophisticated—placed on her hilltop property at, roughly, Sixth and Overland streets. I say "roughly" because Austin surveys of lot placements are somewhat similar to the Amazing Kreskin; nothing is quite as it appears to be. Nonetheless, our double-wide was installed in place of Val's old single-wide, after Kip Helming bulldozed the confining banks a little, and I found I had moved to a VIEW. Not the meager little slice of Reese River Valley visible from my old house on Cedar Street, but a VIEW.

Our brand new trailer hou . . . er, manufactured home was seventy feet long, and since Val had always had her heart set on a full-length deck to better appreciate the spectacular view, I built one. Well, it wasn't quite as simple as "I built one." First I had to design it, and then get the lumber and associated building materials up there, and then put it together. But with that view awaiting, really, what choice did I have?

The dealer assured us that the costs of delivery and set-up were included as part of the price of our new home, and that we could just move in like a family who'd bought a real house. However, as I prepared to build the deck, I found our house had been positioned eight inches lower on one end than it was on the other, which rarely happens with a real house built with a real level. When asked, our dealer said the eight-inch difference was "within acceptable limits," whatever that meant, and at any rate it was too late to complain because we'd already signed off on the deal. Ah. Well. OK. Our bad. But then I was stuck with the thorny problem of how to build a sixty-six-foot-long deck without using a level.

Which brought me full circle. My first two Austin purchases, the Stagecoach Inn and an old house on Cedar Street, were built in the 1800s and as such lacked square corners and perpendicular walls. In order for improvements to blend in, you had to align things by eyeball. If, for instance, you squared up a doorway so it was plumb, it made all the walls look askew, like something out of *Alice in Wonderland*. If you've ever visited the House of Mystery in Oregon, where bottles appear to roll uphill and you can't seem to stand upright because the walls are tilted in different directions, you'll know what I'm talking about. Somebody needs to take a crowbar and do some serious eyeballing up there, and that's how it is with old wooden structures in Austin. That's also how it is with brand-new manufactured housing if you're not careful before you "sign off."

Anyway, I managed to construct a deck that was within acceptable limits, and which blended in with our home, and, as an unexpected bonus, upon which water never puddled. From our deck chairs we had an unparalleled view of Reese River Valley and the mountain ranges beyond, and shade trees Val had fortuitously planted to the west of the yard years before put the finishing touches on perfect summer afternoons. For the past eighteen years we've been treated to spectacular sunsets as well, and I would be hard put to find a finer view on the planet. You could improve on it slightly by climbing into the trees and sitting in the upper branches, which Withanee and I often did, but when company came we stayed pretty much on the deck or in the yard.

Val suggested we build a brick barbecue right on the bank, which would offer the chef an even grander view than the deck. I'd never done masonry work, but what the heck, that's what Sunset do-it-yourself books are for. And brothers-in-law. Not that Rob had a lot of experience in most things— he was too young for that—but once he got interested his willingness and enthusiasm kept projects on track whenever I wandered, as I was wont to do. Also, he lived just down the hill and was ridiculously easy to snag into these things. On this particular project I nearly wept with joy when he told me he'd once helped his father build a brick house back in Kentucky. Whatever misgivings I'd had about the actual brickwork disappeared.

Following Sunset's guidance, we ordered a metal barbecue insert that included two adjustable charcoal trays, and a metal door for a separate storage area. Then I bought a pallet of bricks, some bags of ready-mix mortar, a five-foot level, a couple of trowels, and a large ice chest so we wouldn't have to run back and forth to the house whenever we got thirsty. There. Ready to go. We prepared the forms in which to pour the cement foundation, and then Rob suggested we get a beverage out of the ice chest and take our first break of the morning.

"Is that a great view, or what?" he said, seating himself on the pallet.

"Yes," I replied, looking out at the miniature dust devils swirling out in the valley, "it certainly is."

And there we sat. The vista was mesmerizing. When I built the deck, my back was to the view and I didn't have this problem. But with the barbecue, well, that first day we managed to pour the foundation, and since we had to let it cure overnight before we could lay bricks, we set up a couple of lawn chairs next to the ice chest and watched the sunset.

The following morning we were ready to start in earnest. We mixed a bucket of mortar, and I handed Rob the trowel and a brick. When he handed them back, I pointed out that since he had helped build a brick house in Kentucky he should be the one doing the actual bricklaying. No, he said, the way he'd helped was, he'd handed his father the bricks. Oh.

It was slow going, as bricks don't automatically line up the way you'd think they would, but before the morning was up we had one course of bricks forming a rectangle inside the edge of the foundation, and as a reward we took another break facing the valley. The ice chest and the lawn chairs were proving to be absolutely invaluable. The following day we started on the second course, and as the days ran into weeks and weeks into months, the barbecue began to take shape. Rob and I agreed that the view over the valley was never the same view, although we sat in the same place every single time. It was amazing. Whenever Val or Michelle—our wives—came out, they always seemed to catch us waiting for the mortar to cure, which resulted in La-Z-Boy jokes and another round of beverages, and which may have also slowed construction a bit. But by the time school started, the barbecue project was completed. We celebrated with grilled cheeseburgers and beverages, and it seemed entirely fitting that we all stood around the barbecue enjoying the view. I don't know why we never tired of it.

There are other views around. From Austin Summit south to Dry Creek Road—about eight miles—a dirt road doubles as the Toiyabe Crest Trail along the very top of the ridgeline. The elevation averages around 8,000 feet or a little higher, about 3,000 feet above the valley floor. If you keep going past Dry Creek, they tell me the trail winds up Bunker Hill to an elevation of over 11,000 feet, but I'll take their word for it. You get great vistas of Reese River Valley from the crest road, and to the east you can glimpse Smoky Valley now and then, but ridges spiking out in that direction often get in the way of the view. The top is almost always windblown, ranging from cooling breezes to gales, and you want to make sure your hat's pulled down tight before cresting the ridge. Rob and I rode our motorcycles along the summit trail many times during the summer months, and you dare not gaze around at the views unless you have come to a complete stop. I've said it before and I'll say it again: If you mistake your motorcycle for a tour bus, you're going to leave some hide on the rocks up there. That probably goes for bicycles as well.

If you don't like heights, desert country offers views just as spectacular from the valley floors. There are no pesky trees to block out the surrounding mountain ranges, so you can get a complete 360-degree IMAX-type perspective of the world. When Jean and Jim Hardin—my sister and brother-in-law from Oregon—come to visit, we often drive out into the middle of Reese River Valley and go for long walks with the dogs, just exploring and enjoying the tranquil vastness of it all. It's beautiful out there, and it's not uncommon to come across signs of previous explorers—Shoshone Indians or pioneers or settlers—in the form of obsidian chips or broken glass or rusted metal. On very rare occasions we'll even come across an oxshoe or an old purple bottle or an arrowhead. Jean once found a spur with a large Spanish rowel and moldy remnants of its leather strap. No doubt some old buckaroo got a pretty wild ride out there a century or so ago. I have a lot of pictures of her and Jim holding their treasures up amid the sagebrush in Reese River Valley, but it's not the spurs or the horseshoes that get your attention, it's the uncluttered vastness of the setting.

The very ground they're standing on can also provide goodies. My sister constantly brings back agates and little quartz crystals and other questionable chunks of earth that strike her Oregonian fancy. She'll hold up a chip of granite and say, "Now wouldn't that look pretty with water running over it?" To which Jim replies, "Mm-hmm," and I add "Hmm," and into her bag it goes. It's a lot worse if she spots an appealing one near the jeep, because then she doesn't take size into account. Sometimes it takes both Jim and I to lift it into the back. It is a measure of righteousness that these rocks go to Oregon with Jean and I don't have to worry about stumbling over a new doorstop every year. Val, like me, believes that desert rocks are happy rocks and needn't be bothered. Thank goodness.

In the winter season, the view around Austin is somewhat different; it's white.

The first year we were here, having spent a good part of our respective lives in California, we were reminded that winter is an actual season unto itself. It was much more, um, wintery than we'd thought it would be. Shortly before Marlys and I moved, our local newspaper, the *Antioch Ledger,* ran a front-page story about our impending relocation to central Nevada. Titled "Tiny Nevada Town Lures Local Couple," it delicately skittered around the lunacy of giving up good, much-sought-after jobs in an up-and-coming city to chase after dubious, though admirable, dreams out in the sticks. In it, I'm quoted as saying that when we visited Austin in March, a freak storm had covered the ground with snow. I went on to pontificate that since central Nevada was high desert country, it didn't get much snow. I really believed that, but I don't know why, except maybe that there's so much darn sagebrush around here it doesn't suggest hard winters. Never mind that *Nevada* is Spanish for "snow-covered," as in Sierra Nevada, "snow-covered mountains." It still looks like desert, you know? I don't think many people would blame me for thinking that.

It is pretty. After a snowstorm, the hills and valleys and mountains are blanketed in unblemished white as far as you can see, a vista made even sharper by the clear Arctic-like air. Before I had to work in it, the winter landscape was so enthralling that it made me want to go outside immediately. We tried some of the local outdoor twists to the season, such as tubing. Sledding was a popular winter sport when I was a kid, and I'd heard of tubing before we moved to Austin, but I'd never actually ridden an inner tube down a snowy slope until I got here. Truck tubes were the most popular, because they could hold anywhere from three to five people, depending on the size of both the tube and the people.

The main drawback of an inner tube is that you can't steer it; it follows gravity down the slope no matter how hard you lean or twist or pray. You have exactly two choices, and they are to ride it till it comes to a stop or bail out. Tubing down Virginia Hill was the local answer to Six Flags' coaster rides. It was steep, it was fast, and after it crossed Main Street it started back uphill, which helped tubers slow down before they smacked into the VFW building. The danger was, of course, traffic coming down Main Street. A watcher was always posted at the bottom of Virginia Hill, and nobody would start down until they got the signal that the highway was clear. An irresponsible watcher once amused himself by frantically waving off the sledders in a panicky manner when they were about halfway down, when there really was no traffic, just to watch the resulting explosive bailout and human avalanche. That was awful, and there's just no excuse for that sort of senseless prank. So even though it was the funniest thing I ever saw, I never did it again. And to tell the truth, I never did much tubing either. It was too cold.

We were introduced to Austin's other seasonal pastime by Joe Dory, who came into the ice cream parlor one snowy afternoon and suggested we go ride hoods. Excuse me? Ride hoodlums?

No, dimwit, car hoods.

The dump in Slaughterhouse Canyon used to be a parking lot of scrapped cars, in the days when things like that were called junk and thrown away. The hoods of older cars were streamlined but boxy. If you turned one upside down in the snow it resembled the bed of a shallow wheelbarrow with the back end chopped off, kind of sledlike. Joe hooked one to the back of his four-wheel-drive pickup with a twenty-foot length of chain, thereby creating a circus ride for anyone dumb enough to climb in. I took dibs on the front, where I could face forward and hold on with both hands, like I used to do in boats when Dad took me fishing. Gliding across a lake, pushed by a Sears seven-and-a-half-horsepower outboard motor, it was by far the best seat in the boat, but at 40 MPH across snow it makes you a catcher's mitt for the blizzard roostertailing off the tires.

A couple of miles up Morris Road I was blind, deaf, and . . . er, dumb, cocooned as I was in a compacting layer of ice. Without any sensory input I was unable to help balance the hood when cornering, because I didn't know when or in what direction to lean. All I could do was hang on for dear life as we went whipping back and forth up the winding road. Sadly, I became a detriment as the snow piled up over me, slowly shifting our center of gravity upward. There was maybe a five-minute window when I could have let go and rolled off the back, thereby saving my friends, which would have been the gallant thing to do. In my defense it never crossed my mind. Nothing did.

The spill must have been spectacular, throwing us human snowballs every which way, but the very softness of the snow saved us. I remember the uproarious laughter that rang through the air as I sat there wiping snow from my eyes. Pretty as the view was, and as funny as our predicament was, I recall thinking it would be much funnier and prettier through a window, from the vantage point of a recliner next to the fireplace.

My forays into the more traditional winter sports of skiing and ice-skating resulted in broken ribs and a frantic scramble through bone-chilling water to shore, after the ice broke. After all that, my winter activities could be best described as "nonparticipatory," and remain so to this day.

Apart from the physical views, Austin has provided me with other, more unexpected observations. Had I stayed in California, which was no doubt the wise course, 2006 would probably have been the year in which I retired from my job as a journeyman welder at the paper mill, although I might have worked my way up to maintenance-shop foreman by then. My house would have been paid for long ago, I'd have some really nice cars, probably a boat, maybe a vacation cabin up in the Sierra Nevada foothills—presupposing, of course, that I hadn't killed myself or someone else while driving home from the bar late at night. Not a bad life, all in all. Certainly far better than any I could have hoped for if I hadn't been born in the United States, which, from the very beginning, was an incalculable stroke of genius on my part.

Still, moving to Austin was the best decision I ever made.

For starters, I got to design and build, and even cook in, my very own restaurant, something that everybody wants to do deep down, whether they know it or not. It was a lot of fun, mostly, although the novelty was starting to wear a bit thin even over the relatively short period of time I was involved in it. I also learned about being in business, and I came to appreciate how much this country depends on private businesses, both small and large. In order to serve a cheeseburger deluxe, we dealt with several different wholesalers who supplied us with the meat and the produce and the cheese and the mayonnaise and the pickles and the buns and the potatoes and the napkins and the toothpicks, not to mention those that furnished the propane to cook with and the electricity to run the refrigerators, and the makers of silverware and dishes, etc., etc., etc. The finished product appeared at the narrow end of a very complex funnel of supplies, which had never occurred to me before I experienced it myself.

And although some safeguards naturally need to be in place to protect the consumer, I came to understand that the less governmental interference, whether it be federal, state, or local, the better the system worked and the better the final product was. That was worth a degree in business administration, right there.

I found the same to be true of the temporary jobs I held through the years. The less red tape prospective employers had to cut through to hire me, the better chance I had to go to work, resulting in a lesser chance of my getting into trouble in my spare time, and as an added bonus to society, I could pay more taxes, which helped to start the whole thing all over again. Adding unnecessary fees and inspections and regulations and licensing and taxes just gums up the works and saps energy, making it harder for employers to hire people like me. Not that I'm entirely opposed to that.

My view of police work has changed considerably because of Austin. I think it's safe to say I wouldn't have been hired off the street—or, more accurately, out of the kitchen—and given a badge anywhere else, even back in 1979. Entering law enforcement, I started out with a lot of doubts but soon became impressed with myself and, while standing back to admire my work, lost my first marriage. To make up for it I started drinking heavily on my time off, which of course balanced everything out nicely. By the time I reached what I thought was a happy medium, I had to wait for the dust to settle so I could see to start all over. Well, I owned my own house, although the roof leaked and the windows rattled in the wind, and for some reason I still had a lot of friends in Austin, so things could have been a lot worse. Had I been in a city, I'm sure they would have been a lot worse.

I took a few years off from police work and kicked around a little—you know, remarried, had a child, moved across town, minor things like that— and then I went back into sheriffing with a slightly different perspective. I got back just in time to witness a sea change in law enforcement agencies across the entire nation. In the early 1990s the practice of wearing neckties with winter uniforms disappeared virtually overnight in favor of turtleneck sweaters worn beneath long-sleeved shirts. Highly polished shoes or cowboy boots gave way to combat boots, and baseball caps with the legend POLICE or SHERIFF became standard for active-duty officers everywhere. Uniform styles became much more military, with some departments even blousing their trousers, and mottoes such as "To Protect and Serve" disappeared from the fenders of patrol cruisers. Firearms didn't go untouched either, with traditional six-shot revolvers being replaced by semiautomatic pistols that carried as many as fourteen rounds at a whack.

All this happened without any discernible coordination between agencies or any kind of plan; just poof, and there it was. I still don't know why or how it happened. Much worse, I thought, was the approach being taught to new officers. The primary goal seemed to be one of avoiding liability, of making sure officers didn't open their departments to potential lawsuits, rather than keeping the peace and helping people. That was one revelation I believe I could have done without.

When I became justice of the peace in 1995 I got another surprise. Instead of viewing the defendant as guilty, which I often did as a police officer because I saw the guy do it, I had to view him as innocent once the trial got underway. That wasn't as easy as it sounds, after eleven years as a deputy sheriff. Sitting on the bench was an entirely different kettle of fish, and there were uncomfortable moments when it occurred to me that if I'd made a few more wrong choices and the defendant had made a few more right ones, our roles could easily have been reversed. Most hadn't set out to be defendants any more than I'd set out to be a judge. That didn't stop me from carrying out my sworn duties; the U.S. Marine Corps instilled within me a sense of duty that hadn't diminished in forty years and which served me well as both a deputy and a judge. But it was indeed at times uncomfortable, and the view from the bench was nearly as humbling as the view from the deck.

While attending a course at the National Judicial College, I met Judge Janet Berry from Reno. She had an innovative program she called Kid's Court, in which she invited an elementary school class to her courtroom to actually present a case to a jury of their peers, so they could see how the system worked. It wasn't unstructured; the kids were assigned roles and had scripts to follow throughout the proceedings. But then the jury were given their instructions and sequestered until they reached an unscripted verdict. Janet lent the program to me, because this was my kind of hearing, as even I had a preprinted dialogue. My wife's combined third-and-fourth-grade class was picked for the task, and they wholeheartedly fell to, with parents making costumes and helping their kids learn the lines. The jury took up a good part of the rest of the school.

On the date of the trial, Austin Justice Court was filled nearly to capacity with spectators, which was something the courtroom hadn't seen since the 1800s. When my bailiff, a serious, mustachioed little fellow wearing a sheriff's badge on his Red Ryder vest, called for the audience to rise, I had serious doubts that I was going to be able to get through this, even with a script. The plaintiff, B. B. Wolf (the initials standing for "Big Bad," naturally), was seated next to his nattily dressed attorney, and the defendant, Curly Pig, was seated next to hers. Miss Pig, whom I recognized as my daughter behind the plastic snout and floppy ears, was being sued for injuries received by Mr. Wolf—who faintly resembled Billy Gandolfo beneath the wolfish mask—when he dropped from her chimney into a pot of scalding water she had sitting in the fireplace. It was a tragic story, as Curly's brothers, Larry and Moe, had already been the victims of "porkicide" during prior suspicious house-collapsing incidents. What a tale. What a trial. What a day. The jury eventually found in favor of Curly Pig, the courtroom erupted in applause at the dismissal of the case, and I made it back to my chambers in a somewhat judgly manner, although it was a very near thing. The kids' view of our judicial system changed that day, and darned if mine didn't, also. Never again would I consider any testimony trivial.

Between sheriffing and judging, it became obvious to me that my high school literature teacher had it all wrong; almost everything in life is indeed black or white, right or wrong, good or evil, and his "varying shades of gray" theory needs to be scrapped, because it really clutters up the view.

There are three active churches in Austin, the most historical being the Episcopal church on Main Street. A much newer structure houses the Church of Latter-day Saints up the street, and the Baptist church meets in their building above Main Street overlooking the town park. None of them gets as much business as you'd think, living out here. Left to my own devices I doubt they'd have had my business either, even though my wife and daughter attended the Baptist church from the time Withanee was a toddler. I can't give Austin any credit for propelling me into church, because that came from a much higher power, but I can say the setting has made it a more pleasant experience than what I recall of my sporadic church attendance in the city. As in all things Austin, the scope is smaller here. You know everybody, of course, which makes it seem more of a family gathering than a congregation. There are also additional services and kids' activities on Wednesday evenings, a potluck lunch the first Sunday of the month, Easter sunrise services on Bob Scott Summit every year, a revival each summer, and a regional Snowfest every winter. On Sunday Loretta leads the singing, Joan plays the piano, Bill accompanies on the guitar, and Pastor Ron Barney unfailingly delivers a dynamic sermon just after Susie leads the kids in Children's Church. Can you get any more down-home that that? Oh, and parking is a breeze, if you choose to drive rather than walk. Which we do. All in all, I don't know that churchgoing is better here than in a city, but I do know it's a whole lot more fun.

As I write this it's springtime in Austin, and I'm having an awful time getting off the deck. The view across the valley, framed between the V of my feet propped up on the handrail, seems a little different than it was last year. It's hard to put my finger on it, but it's also pleasantly distracting.

Maybe that just about sums up life in Austin.

WINDING DOWN

When the county seat was whisked away to Battle Mountain, it was predicted that Austin would become a genuine ghost town within a decade. At about the same time, it was also predicted that the Alaska pipeline would cause caribou to become extinct. The caribou, I think, did better than we did—they are absolutely flourishing—but Austin is doing all right. It is such a beautiful town, in such a beautiful setting, that I don't see how it could ever die, but then I'm sure that's been said before of different towns in different times, many of which have been reduced to rock ruins baking in the Nevada sun. I don't even know if that's possible anymore; given today's degree of legislative meddling, it may be against the law.

For a while, however, after Kent's Market closed down, things did start looking a little bleak on Main Street. Our bank was long gone, the Stagecoach Inn was already boarded up, and then Clara's Golden Club closed, and then Ramos's Chevron shut down. On the bright side, there was no problem finding a parking place.

The *Reno Gazette-Journal* ran a comprehensive commentary on Austin that covered three full pages, later included in a coffee-table book on Nevada, and it came out sounding an awful lot like an obituary.

Then Mitch Cantrell, apparently unfazed by the noticeable decline along Main Street, opened a turquoise-and-jewelry shop below the International Cafe. Shortly after, Jim Graham moved to Austin and bought Ramos's station. He refurbished the outside and expanded the inside to include the area where gas pumps used to stand. Renamed the Trading Post, it offers gifts and Nevada memorabilia. Phillip and Joan Williams joined in with the Nevada Blue jewelry store between the Pony Canyon and Lincoln motels. Another family with former ties to the area, the Marshals, bought some old buildings along Main Street and put in the lavishly equipped but poorly designed Silver State Bar and Grill, along with a barbershop and a museum. Truth to tell, the Marshal enterprises haven't worked out, but they very well may in the future. The Marshals have also come up with a design for a town square, where the old Austin Hotel used to stand, that looks promising. Jan Morrison opened the Main Street Shops and also acquired the Stagecoach Inn, which she plans to reopen soon. Elizabeth Rassiga now owns the nineteenth-century boardinghouse known as the Leland House and is remodeling it along with the adjoining structures. The owners of the Toiyabe Cafe, Jenni and Ray Williams, have spruced up the building and repaved the parking lot with paving stones, which gives the place a nice Old World look. Up the street, the old Forest Service building is being turned into a new museum, across the highway from which Tom White has opened Tom's Treasures, a curio shop of Nevada offerings.

These are just the Main Street improvements; if you drive the back streets you'll see a lot of remodeling activity that is undoubtedly related to what's going on downtown. If I didn't know better, I'd say Austin might be on the threshold of a comeback, but I don't think those of us who've seen both the booms and the busts are really going to be surprised by anything that happens around here. Austin, which seems at first glance like a changeless little place modeled after a snow-village paperweight, is anything but. That is where the surprise lies.

Things are changing even faster for Val and me because our only daughter graduates from high school this year. Withanee will be attending college starting in August, and she'll be taking with her the skills she's honed in Austin. Those skills aren't city skills, but we think—and hope—they're adaptable to her new life and that she'll do fine. More than Withanee, I think, it is Val and I who will have to learn to adapt to our new lives in Austin. For the past twelve years we've centered most of our time around school events, such as traveling to away games on weekends to the tune of several thousand miles. And even before that our lives revolved around kids, and kids' games, and kids' vacations, and kids' parties, and kids' books, and kids' pets. It was a great, great time.

However, now that we've finished all the hard work, I think I've earned the right to finally break down and do what I've always wanted to do—buy me a nice fresh bag of circus peanuts, sit out on the deck in a lounge chair, and indulge myself in composing literature for the ages, or at least the *Reese River Reveille*. And look at that view, would you?

Man, it just doesn't get any better than this.